ESG IN THE INSURANCE MARKETS OF CENTRAL ASIA

Lessons from Uzbekistan

R U S T A M   A Z I M O V
Uzbekinvest, Uzbekistan

ESG IN THE INSURANCE MARKETS OF CENTRAL ASIA

Lessons from Uzbekistan

World Scientific

NEW JERSEY • LONDON • SINGAPORE • BEIJING • SHANGHAI • HONG KONG • TAIPEI • CHENNAI • TOKYO

Published by

World Scientific Publishing Co. Pte. Ltd.
5 Toh Tuck Link, Singapore 596224
USA office: 27 Warren Street, Suite 401-402, Hackensack, NJ 07601
UK office: 57 Shelton Street, Covent Garden, London WC2H 9HE

Library of Congress Control Number: 2025047185

British Library Cataloguing-in-Publication Data
A catalogue record for this book is available from the British Library.

ESG IN THE INSURANCE MARKETS OF CENTRAL ASIA
Lessons from Uzbekistan

ISBN 978-981-98-2217-1 (hardcover)
ISBN 978-981-98-2218-8 (ebook for institutions)
ISBN 978-981-98-2219-5 (ebook for individuals)

For any available supplementary material, please visit
https://www.worldscientific.com/worldscibooks/10.1142/14555#t=suppl

Desk Editors: Eshak Nabi Akbar Ali/Geysilla Jean Ortiz

Typeset by Stallion Press
Email: enquiries@stallionpress.com

Printed in Singapore

About the Author

Rustam Sadikovich Azimov is a prominent Uzbek economist. He graduated from Tashkent State University and the Tashkent Institute of Irrigation and Melioration, earning degrees as an economist-engineer. From 1980 to 1984, he served as a lecturer at Tashkent State University and, in 1984, defended his dissertation to earn a PhD in economics at the Tashkent State University of Economics. Following this, he worked as an economist and chief economist at agricultural enterprises in Uzbekistan from 1984 to 1988, before returning to academia to teach economics at higher education institutions until 1990.

Azimov has had a distinguished career in both finance and politics in Uzbekistan. In 1990–1991, he founded and served as chairman of the board of the newly established private commercial bank "Ipak Yuli." From 1991 to 1998, he served as the chairman of the board of the newly established National Bank for Foreign Economic Activity of the Republic of Uzbekistan. His political career advanced significantly when he held various ministerial positions from 1998 to 2017, including Minister of Finance, Minister of Economy, and Minister of Foreign Economic Affairs and Investment, while also serving as Deputy Prime Minister and First Deputy Prime Minister.

Between 1992 and 2017, Azimov represented Uzbekistan as governor at several international financial institutions, including the International Monetary Fund, the World Bank, the Asian Development Bank, and the European Bank for Reconstruction and Development. Since 2017, he has been the general director of the export–import insurance company Uzbekinvest. In 2022, he furthered his academic credentials by defending his dissertation for the degree of doctor of science in economics at the Tashkent State University of Economics. His expertise in economics and finance has been instrumental in shaping Uzbekistan's economic policies over the years.

In addition to his financial expertise, Azimov has authored over 50 scientific works, including five monographs published internationally. His latest book, *Transformation of the Insurance Business in Countries with Transition Economies (Based on Uzbekistan Experience)*, was published by Proud Pen Publishing House in 2024. This work highlights the challenges and opportunities in adapting insurance practices to meet the needs of a modernizing economy. He has also co-authored eight collective monographs and authored over 60 academic papers on insurance and modern technology.

His academic contributions have enriched the field of economics and finance, showcasing his keen insights and innovative approaches, particularly in the context of Uzbekistan's evolving economy. His work often focuses on the modernization of financial systems and the development of insurance mechanisms to protect property interests in a transitioning economy. His publications, such as those on IPO placements and integrated quality management systems, demonstrate a deep understanding of financial stability, investor attraction, and business performance. These topics are highly relevant and could attract readers interested in practical applications and case studies. He has been recognized for his contributions with awards such as the Order of Mehnat Shuhrati in 1998 and Fidokorona Xizmatlar Uchun in 2008.

Contents

Introduction

The deeper digitalization and automation penetrate all areas of the insurance business, the more theories arise for further socio-economic development of the local insurance market. The insurance market in Uzbekistan is operating under unique conditions – along with automation processes implemented with the widespread introduction of Insurtech mechanisms specific to the Fourth Industrial Revolution (Industry 4.0), artificial intelligence applications are increasing in number, involving the interaction of human and machine and digital insurance transformation.

At the same time, human–machine systems are a sign of Industry 5.0, characterized by synergy between people and robotic systems. Thus, in the insurance practices of Uzbekistan, Industry 4.0 – automation of basic technological processes – smoothly flows into Industry 5.0 – the digital transformation of the insurance business, where individuals are either completely excluded from the technological processes of providing insurance services or interact with digital technologies to a significant extent. In turn, these processes overlap the economy transformation processes as a whole – the processes of formation of a socially oriented market economy.

Under the conditions of a transitional economy, when changes in political, social, and economic structures take place with high intensity, the principles of sustainable development become especially relevant. Environmental, social, and governance (ESG) factors, which initially emerged as tools for assessing corporate responsibility and sustainability, currently play a key role in the process of adaptation and transformation of various industries, including the insurance industry.

The insurance industry, being at the intersection of the financial sector and the real economy, faces unique challenges in the process of integrating ESG principles. In countries with transition economies, these challenges are further intensified by market volatility, legislative changes, and socio-economic transformations. Implementing ESG standards in such conditions requires not only a deep analysis of current risks but also the development of new strategies that contribute to increasing the sustainability and competitiveness of insurance companies.

Sustainable development is a key concept of modern insurance, which implies a balance of three components – environment, economy, and society – ESG strategies. In this case, the abbreviation "ESG" can be spelled out as "environmental, social, and governance". In a broad sense, it is the sustainable development of commercial activity, which is based on the following principles: A responsible attitude to the environment (E – environmental); high social responsibility (S – social); and high quality of corporate governance (G – governance).

The relevance of the ESG agenda for insurance businesses is confirmed by international experience: The number of companies that have signed the Principles for Sustainable

Insurance (PSI), formulated 12 years ago, has grown from 180 to 265 (including 159 signatory and 106 supporting companies) from 50 countries since 2022. The total asset value of these companies now exceeds US$15 trillion, and the volume of premiums earned by these companies is 30% of the global insurance market.[1]

The basic principles of PSI can be summarized as follows. It is necessary:

- to take into account the ESG factors in the decision-making process;
- to raise awareness among clients and business partners of the ESG criteria for risk management and decision-making;
- to work with government bodies and stakeholders on ESG issues;
- to publish regular reports on the progress of the implementation of the principles.

The insurance business has the potential not only to provide guarantees to minimize the risks of its clients but also to develop the entire society as a whole and ensure its sustainable development. At the same time, insurance companies directly depend on the trust placed in them and the loyalty of the consumers of insurance services. Therefore, building relationships with clients and reputational risks form the basis for the sustainable development of insurance companies.

Insurance organizations can achieve sustainable success through effective management, awareness of the organization's environment, learning, and the proper application of innovations and improvements. To maintain it, it is necessary to regularly monitor the organization's environment, study and analyze the effectiveness of its activities, and evaluate the achievement of the set results in accordance with the mission, vision, policy, strategy, and goals of the organization.

Today, the insurance development in Uzbekistan is gaining national significance. The state is currently striving to not be the main source of insurance provision. Therefore, the organization of insurance guarantees systems on market conditions, ahead of insurance services development provided by non-state insurance companies, is in demand and is a particularly significant element of a full-fledged modern business environment in the Republic of Uzbekistan. The presence of the above-mentioned circumstances predetermines the relevance of the topic of this monograph.

It should be noted that despite the research and scientific studies carried out in practice, theoretical, methodological, and individual practical issues related to the implementation and further development of the ESG agenda in the domestic insurance market are not comprehensively covered. This situation further increases the relevance of the scientific and applied issues presented in the monograph, as well as proposals and recommendations for their elimination.

The scientific significance of the research results presented in the monograph is determined by the possibility of using them both to improve the ESG strategies of domestic insurers and in scientific research conducted in our country and aimed at the scientific and theoretical development of disciplines such as: "insurance theory", "insurance business", "insurance management", and "riskology".

The practical significance of the research results lies in the development of methodological foundations for regulatory documents and programs of activities aimed at the implementation and further development of ESG strategies by local insurers.

---

[1] https://www.ra-national.ru/analitika/integracija-principov-esg-v-strahovoj-otrasli-v-mire-rastet-dolja-strahovanija-ot-katastrof-v-svjazi-s-izmeneniem-klimata-v-rossii-rasshirjaetsja-kolichestvo-produktov-s-jekologicheskoj-sostavljajushh/.

The first chapter of the monograph examines the features of the emerging economy of the Central Asian states, analyzes research in the field of transition economies in the Central Asian countries, and identifies common features and key differences in the economic models of the Central Asian countries.

The second chapter of the monograph is devoted to the issues of ESG transformation in the insurance business, considering the economic essence and goals of such transformation. Considerable attention is paid to theoretical issues of integrating ESG principles into the activities of domestic insurers, and the need for advanced development of state regulation of ESG processes in the insurance market of the republic is justified.

The third chapter of the monograph provides an in-depth study of the ESG transformation methodology of the insurance business, including the ESG transformation of the insurer itself and the insurance market as a whole, and considers the basic principles of such transformation. Consideration of the issues of the ESG transformation methodology of the insurance business is due to the need to systematize the accumulated experience, clarify the formulations, and develop a corresponding thesaurus.

Innovative aspects of ESG transformation of the insurance business are considered in the fourth chapter of the monograph. It also studies the prospects for digital transformation of the domestic insurance market and the main inclusive priorities (human-centricity) of the insurance business development. Particular attention is paid to the prospects of "green" insurance in Uzbekistan.

The issues and prospects for ESG transformation of insurance in Uzbekistan are studied in the fifth chapter of the monograph. The current state of the insurance market in the republic is considered from the point of view of readiness for ESG transformation and the role of ESG transformation of insurance in achieving Uzbekistan's national Sustainable Development Goals; the concept of ESG transformation of the domestic insurance business is also proposed.

This monograph is devoted to the study of the ESG transformation process in the insurance industry in conditions of a transition economy. It examines specific aspects related to the implementation of ESG principles in insurance activities in the context of structural changes, analyzes both new risks and opportunities arising in these conditions, and offers recommendations for effective management and adaptation to new challenges. The monograph can be used by researchers, postgraduate and master's students, and specialists in insurance companies when studying issues of ESG transformation of the domestic insurance business.

It should be noted that a number of scientific and methodological provisions of the monograph are of a debatable nature, so the author would be grateful for any comments and suggestions, which can be sent to the following address: office@uzbekinvest.uz.

Chapter 1

Specifics of the Transition Economy of the Central Asian States

1.1 Research Analysis in the Field of Transition Economies in Central Asian Countries

The economic role of Central Asian countries in the global context continues to be the subject of active research and debate among experts in international economics and political science. Despite the region's important geographical location, playing a key role in trade routes between East and West, its economic significance and development prospects have not yet received due attention in the world scientific literature. Central Asian countries such as Kazakhstan, Uzbekistan, Kyrgyzstan, Tajikistan, and Turkmenistan started economic transformation after the collapse of the Soviet Union in 1991, which became an important stage in both their political and economic evolution.

With the transition from the planned economies of the Soviet era to market economies, the Central Asian countries have faced a number of unique challenges that reflect both the specificities of the region and broader trends common to post-Soviet states. In conditions of significant economic changes accompanied by the privatization of state enterprises, foreign trade liberalization, financial reforms, and globalization, these states have begun to develop strategies aimed at stimulating economic growth, diversifying their economies, and integrating into international economic and trade structures.

An important aspect of these reforms was the attempt to build effective market mechanisms in conditions of insufficient institutional maturity, low transparency, and limited development of financial markets. Despite this, the Central Asian countries demonstrated high growth rates in a number of key sectors, such as energy, agriculture, and metallurgy, as well as in some information technology and services sectors. For example, Kazakhstan has become the largest hydrocarbon exporter in the region, and Uzbekistan has begun to implement agricultural reforms aimed at improving food security and developing agribusiness.

Natural resources play a special role in the economic progress of the Central Asian countries, significantly influencing economic development and geopolitical strategy. The presence of large reserves of hydrocarbons and precious metals, as well as a strategic location at the intersection of major trade routes, provides these states with competitive advantages in international markets. At the same time, dependence on natural resource exports makes the region's economy vulnerable to price fluctuations on world markets and economic crises, underlining the need for the diversification and development of non-resource sectors.

In addition, Central Asian states are actively seeking to deepen economic cooperation with neighboring countries and world powers. Regional initiatives such as the creation of the Eurasian Economic Union, as well as participation in Chinese initiatives such as the Belt and Road Initiative, demonstrate the desire of Central Asian countries not only to strengthen their economic security but also to integrate into global production chains.

However, despite the progress made, the countries of the region continue to face a number of structural and institutional challenges that prevent further development. These include high corruption levels, insufficient legal protection of property, and weak financial institutions, as well as inequality and poverty in some countries. Effective overcoming of these obstacles will require deep institutional reforms, improved governance, and sustainable economic growth.

The research analysis in the field of transition economies in Central Asian countries is an important and multifaceted task since this topic covers the complex processes of transformation of economies that were once part of the centrally planned system into market economies. Research in this area began to actively develop after the Soviet Union's collapse, and over several decades, an extensive scientific base has been formed that helps to better understand the specifics of the transition period, challenges, and prospects for the countries of the region.

Various theoretical approaches aimed at studying transition economies are widely discussed in the scientific literature. One of the central concepts is the "transition economy" concept, characterized by changes from a centralized planned economy to market mechanisms. Researchers analyzing the countries of Central Asia rely on theories of economic reforms, such as the theory of shock therapy, gradual reforms, and theories of institutional change.

Shock therapy involves rapid and radical measures aimed at price liberalization, privatization, and the establishment of market institutions. However, this approach has been criticized for its severe social consequences, such as increased poverty and unemployment.

Gradual reforms focus on a more cautious approach that takes into account the need to gradually introduce market mechanisms. This approach has been more common in Central Asia, where many countries have chosen "hybrid" reform strategies.

A key element of the transition in Central Asian countries was the shift in the institutional structure of the economy. Research shows that the success of economic reforms largely depended on the organization and strengthening of such institutions as the legal system, labor market, financial institutions, and corporate governance systems. One of the main problems was the lack of institutional maturity, especially in conditions of weak legal protection and high corruption levels.

Kazakhstan was one of the first countries in Central Asia to implement a number of radical reforms as part of shock therapy aimed at rapid liberalization of the economy. The main measures taken as part of shock therapy were as follows:

Price liberalization: In 1992, Kazakhstan took drastic steps to liberalize prices for goods and services, which not only caused inflation and increased social tensions but also accelerated the transition to a market economy.

Privatization: Mass privatization of state enterprises, including large industrial facilities, was one of the main elements of shock therapy. This process was often accompanied by significant social and economic consequences since the new private owners of the enterprises often had great political and economic leverage.

Currency stabilization and financial reform: In 1993, the tenge was introduced as the national currency of Kazakhstan, followed by the introduction of tough economic measures aimed at stabilizing the currency market and fighting hyperinflation.

These measures led to a sharp economic downturn, rising unemployment, and social tensions, but they also laid the foundations for further economic growth in the later period.

Unlike Kazakhstan, Uzbekistan in the first years of independence followed a more "gradual" approach to reform, avoiding the abrupt steps of shock therapy. However, some elements of shock therapy were also applied in the country, especially in the areas of price liberalization and foreign trade.

In the early 1990s, Uzbekistan faced the need to implement reforms, including price liberalization and creating conditions for private entrepreneurs to operate. However, these processes were much softer than in Kazakhstan, and the government carried them out more carefully to avoid economic collapse.

Although privatization processes were introduced in Uzbekistan, they were carried out more slowly than in Kazakhstan. This allowed the authorities to maintain control over key sectors of the economy, which was part of a strategy of gradual reforms.

Turkmenistan and Tajikistan have retained economic governance forms characterized by greater state control.

Kyrgyzstan has been more oriented towards liberalization and privatization, becoming the first state to significantly privatize its assets in the 1990s.

Research in this area highlights the importance of establishing functional institutions, such as independent judiciaries and competitive markets, to ensure long-term growth and sustainability of the economy. In the Central Asian context, research also focuses on the challenges of adapting old governance systems and the interaction of new market institutions with traditional power structures.

The Central Asian economies in the post-Soviet period are an example of a complex and multifaceted process of transition from a centrally planned economy to market mechanisms. Despite some success, the region's path to sustainable and diversified economic development remains far from complete. Current and future research in this area is necessary for a thorough understanding of both local and global processes influencing the economic future of Central Asia.

Overall, the literature on this region is characterized by its diversity of approaches, its focus on different transition aspects, and its in-depth analysis of both theoretical and empirical data. However, despite significant achievements, it also faces a number of limitations and challenges that are important to consider when analyzing it. Table 1.1 presents the results of the literature analysis on transition economies in Central Asia.

An analysis of the above table shows that the strengths of the research into transition economies in Central Asian countries lie in the diversity of approaches, the availability of empirical data, and the ability to analyze key aspects of economic transition, such as financial reforms, the state role, institutional changes, and external economic integration.

The limitations of many studies are related to the insufficient consideration of sociocultural factors, the specifics of individual countries in the region, and the predominance of macroeconomic approaches over a deeper analysis of the social and political environment.

Research into the transition economies of Central Asian countries covers a wide range of issues, from theoretical models of economic reforms to specific socio-economic issues. Despite significant achievements, the countries of the region continue to face a number of problems, such as insufficient institutional maturity, problems with social stability, and dependence on natural resources. However, successful examples of reforms and economic growth in some Central Asian countries confirm that the right combination of domestic policy, external economic integration, and institutional transformations can lead to sustainable development in the future. Despite the research and theoretical studies that have been carried out in practice, issues related to the characteristics and challenges of Central Asian countries have not been sufficiently studied.

Table 1.1. Results of the research analysis in the field of transition economy type in the countries of Central Asia.

Author(s)/Work	Main Topics and Approaches	Research Methods	Strong Sides	Limitations and Critics
Stiglitz, J. E. (2002). Globalization and Its Discontents	The impact of globalization and international financial organizations on the countries of Central Asia.	Theoretical analysis, criticism of IMF and World Bank programs.	Strong theoretical basis, critical view on globalization.	Insufficient attention to local context and internal factors in the countries of the region.
Rajan, R. G. and Zingales, L. (2003). The Capitalistic Spirit	The role of capitalism and market reforms in transition economies.	Theoretical research, comparative analysis of different countries.	Universal approach, attention to the institutional environment.	Does not consider the peculiarities of regional cultures and political context.
Grigoriev, G. (1999). Economic Reforms in the CIS Countries: The Challenges of Transition	Analysis of economic reforms in the CIS countries, including Central Asia.	Empirical analysis of post-Soviet reforms, statistical data.	Extensive coverage of post-Soviet countries, comprehensive approach.	Generalizations may not take into account differences among Central Asian countries.
Lahti, M. L. (2002). Transition and Institutional Change in Central Asia	Institutional changes and their impact on transition to a market economy.	Qualitative research, interviews with experts, analysis of the political and economic environment.	In-depth analysis of institutional changes in Central Asia.	Insufficient attention to the social and cultural components of reforms.
Shymberdiyev, K. (2006). The Economic Transition of Kazakhstan: Challenges and Opportunities	Features of the transition economy of Kazakhstan, the role of state regulation.	Case analysis, statistical analysis.	Focus on Kazakhstan, detailed macroeconomic analysis.	The application of the findings to other Central Asian countries is limited.
Rakhimov, S. (2004). Economic Reform and the Role of Government in Central Asia	The state's role in the transition to a market economy.	Comparative analysis of state reforms in different countries of the region.	Attention to the state role, emphasis on regulatory policies.	Little attention has been paid to internal political and social conflicts.
Baek, P. (2001). Economic Reforms and Financial Stability in Central Asia: A Comparative Analysis	Economic reforms and financial stabilization in the countries of Central Asia.	Comparative analysis, data from financial institutions.	Detailed analysis of the financial sector, cross-country comparison.	Limited focus on the financial sector, ignores the social sphere.
Kasyimov, A. (2003). Economic Growth and Structural Transformation in Central Asia	Economic growth and its relationship with structural changes in Central Asia.	Statistical analysis, economic growth modeling.	Good coverage of structural change and growth in Kazakhstan and Uzbekistan.	Limited data on less developed countries in the region (Tajikistan and Kyrgyzstan).

Kaufmann, D., Kraay, A. and Mastruzzi, M. (2009). Governance Matters VII	The impact of the public administration quality on the economy of Central Asian countries.	Indicators of management quality, statistical data.	A wide range of indicators, objective assessment of state institutions.	Limited in the context of Central Asian countries, does not consider local political conditions.
Rashid, A. (2002). The Resurgence of Central Asia: Islam, Nationalism, and Politics	The impact of islamization and nationalism on the economy and politics of Central Asia.	Qualitative methods, historical and political analysis.	Analysis of political and economic processes, influence of cultural factors.	Limited economic perspective, emphasis on politics and culture.
Cummings, S. N. and Lewis, A. (2003). Post-Soviet Economic Reforms in Central Asia: A Case Study Approach	Comparative analysis of post-Soviet economic reforms in Central Asia.	Case method, empirical research in each country.	A variety of examples, a variety of approaches to reform.	Deeper macroeconomic links and interactions may be missed.
Aslund, A. (2007). How Russia Became a Market Economy	Analysis of Russia's transition to a market economy and its analogies for Central Asia.	Comparative analysis of the transition in Russia and Central Asia.	A clear and accessible presentation of the market reform process.	Insufficient attention to regions with fewer resources, such as Tajikistan and Kyrgyzstan.
Pomfret, R. (2006). The Economics of Central Asia	A comprehensive analysis of transition economies of Central Asia, with an emphasis on foreign trade and integration into global markets.	Econometric analysis, review of macroeconomic indicators.	An integrated approach, including foreign economic integration.	Insufficient consideration of the socio-political aspects of economic transition.
Davies, P. and Ginsburg, N. (2000). Financial Sector Reform in Central Asia	Issues of financial stabilization and reform of financial systems in Central Asia.	Empirical analysis, data on financial markets and institutions.	Good overview of the financial systems state, emphasis on stabilization.	Underestimating the social consequences of financial reforms.
Alesina, A. and Spolaore, E. (2003). The Size of Nations	The influence of country size and the international labor division on economic development.	Theoretical analysis, research on globalization.	Theoretical contribution, research of economic and political factors.	Not always applicable to specifics of Central Asia, where political and social factors play a key role.

Source: Developed by the author based on the analysis of available literature.

1.2 Specific Features of Economic Systems of Central Asian Countries

The economic systems of the Central Asian countries possess a number of specific features due to the complex interaction of historical, economic, natural, political, and social factors. Central Asia, including Kazakhstan, Uzbekistan, Turkmenistan, Kyrgyzstan, and Tajikistan (Fig. 1.1), is a region where the development of economic systems cannot be considered outside the context of historical and political evolution, as well as the natural and cultural traditions specific to this region. The world has not yet fully realized the economic role and development prospects of the Central Asian countries.

The states of the region have achieved significant progress in their development over the past 20 years and have serious growth prospects. The region's GDP has grown by an average of 6.2% in real terms annually over the past 20 years and reached US$347 billion. The population of Central Asia is almost 77 million people and continues to grow at 2% annually. The volume of accumulated inward investment from third countries is estimated at US$211 billion, and foreign trade turnover has increased sixfold since 2000. The achievements and structural changes in the region are presented in Table 1.2. However, due to inertia, the region is not yet perceived by the international community as a significant player on the world economic map.[1]

The countries of the region have received a historic chance to take advantage of their transit location, as well as opportunities to access foreign markets through emerging international transport corridors. Significant opportunities are related to the coordinated development of the water and energy complex, including "green" energy. To unlock the region's potential, it is important to overcome other challenges, such as lack of access to the sea, resource dependence, low financial development levels, and the impact of climate change.

Fig. 1.1. Central Asian states.[2]

[1]Economy of Central Asia: A New Look. https://eabr.org/upload/iblock/d0b/EDB_2022_Report-3_The-Economy-of-CA_rus.pdf.

[2]https://www.orexca.com/rus/central-asia.htm.

Table 1.2. Achievements and structural changes in the region.

No.	Indicator Name	2000	2010	2021	2023	Growth (× times)
1.	Population, million people	55	62	77	79.3	1.4
2.	GDP, billion USD	46	243	347	384.2	7.5
3.	Share of world GDP at PPP, %	0.4	0.6	0.7	0.8	1.8
4.	Total FDI volume, billion USD	12.3	101.6	211.4	230.6	17.2
5.	Foreign trade goods turnover, billion dollars	27.4	149.4	165.5	180.6	6

Source: Developed by the author based on data from the national statistical agencies, central (national) banks, IMF, ADB, WB, Trademap, and CEIC.

The strategic role of the Central Asian states in the vast Eurasian space will increase, reflecting the region's importance for its closest neighbors and key economic partners, Russia and China. The strategies of the Central Asian countries are based on using the advantages of globalization and regional economic integration in a transition economy. A transition economy is a type of economy that is in the process of transformation from one economic system to another, usually from a centrally planned economy to a market economy. This process is often accompanied by significant changes in the country's politics, economy, social structure, and legal system.

The transition period can be followed by economic instability, high inflation, unemployment, and inequality. However, successful transitions can lead to sustainable economic growth and an increase in the standard of living of the population.

A transition economy possesses a number of specific features that distinguish it from other economic systems. These features are discussed in the following sections.

1.2.1 *Building reliable modern legislative systems and mechanisms for enforcing the transition*

During the economic transition, considerable issues with the legal system are often observed, including insufficient development of the legal framework for protecting businesses and private property. These problems can significantly complicate investment attraction and stifle private sector development. One of the main reasons is the lack of sufficient legal transparency, as well as weak property rights protection, leading to a decrease in investor confidence and preventing sustainable economic growth.

In order to effectively address the existing issues in the legal system, it is necessary to carry out comprehensive measures aimed at strengthening judicial independence and improving law enforcement mechanisms. In particular, it is important to ensure the creation of a legal environment where the judiciary will function impartially and without external interference. This will ensure the stability of legal norms and increase investor confidence, which, in turn, will create conditions for active business development and attract foreign investment.

Strengthening judicial independence and improving law enforcement mechanisms are necessary steps to build an effective legal system that can support the functioning of the private sector and promote sustainable economic development.

1.2.2 *Creating and developing market infrastructure and its main institutions*

For the functioning of a market economy, certain institutions are required, such as banks and insurance companies; commodity, currency, and stock exchanges; tax and customs systems; and antimonopoly authorities and legal incentives to protect property rights. In transition economies, these institutions are often not yet developed or are in the process of being established. The Soviet planning system left deep traces in the economic structure of the newly independent states of Central Asia and the Caucasus. State-owned enterprises dominated industry, agriculture, and services, often with low efficiency and high dependence on subsidies.

During the transition period, the organization of market institutions often faces problems of a lack of qualified personnel and technical infrastructure. The effectiveness of reforms largely depends on the speed and quality of the organization of these institutions. Efforts are also required to educate and train specialists to ensure the normal functioning of financial markets and regulatory bodies.

1.2.3 *Price liberalization*

In planned economies, prices are often set by the state. During the transition period, prices are liberalized, i.e. their regulation is left to the market. This can lead to a significant increase in prices for many goods and services.

Price liberalization can have both positive and negative consequences. On the one hand, it can stimulate competition and improve the quality of goods and services. On the other hand, a sudden increase in prices can lead to social discontent and protests, especially among the most vulnerable groups in the population. To mitigate these consequences, the state may need to introduce social support measures.

1.2.4 *Privatization and private sector development*

In a transition economy, there is a shift from state ownership of the means of production to private ownership. Privatization can take various forms, such as the sale of state enterprises to private investors or the distribution of shares among the population. Privatization is often accompanied by difficulties related to the management and control of the process. This can lead to corruption and non-transparent transactions. To increase the privatization effectiveness, it is important to ensure transparency of procedures and create mechanisms for monitoring the implementation of reforms. The privatization process in individual countries of the region was often accompanied by inefficient distribution of assets, which contributed to the emergence of oligarchic structures and the concentration of wealth in the hands of a limited number of people.

1.2.5 *Reforming the banking and financial systems*

In a transition economy, it is necessary to form a financial system capable of providing credit to the private sector and managing cash flows. This includes the development of commercial banks, a central bank, stock markets, and insurance companies.

Effective reform of the banking system requires strengthening financial supervision and the introduction of international financial reporting standards. This will help to strengthen confidence in financial institutions and improve their ability to lend to the private sector.

1.2.6 *Changing the structure of the economy*

A transition economy is characterized by a shift in the structure of production and consumption.

Azerbaijan, Kazakhstan, and Turkmenistan are major producers of oil and gas. These resources are the main sources of income, but they also create dependence on demand fluctuations and world energy prices.

Uzbekistan and Kyrgyzstan have significant reserves of gold, uranium, and other minerals. This creates opportunities for economic growth but also imposes risks related to the environmental and social impacts of extraction.

Tajikistan and Kyrgyzstan have significant hydropower potential.

Planned economies typically place a strong emphasis on heavy industry and the public sector, while market economies retain a certain share of heavy industry and shift their focus to services and small businesses, implementing sustainable practices in resource extraction and other sectors to minimize environmental impacts and enhance corporate social responsibility.

An urgent challenge for the countries of the region is to stimulate the growth of sectors such as information technology, tourism, the agro-industrial complex, and manufacturing in order to reduce dependence on raw materials. The transition period may also be accompanied by a change in the employment structure, where high technology and service sectors begin to play a more significant role. This requires educational reforms and workforce retraining programs.

1.2.7 *Gradual integration into the global economy*

Transition economies often seek to integrate into the global economy through trade, foreign investment, and participation in international organizations, such as the World Trade Organization (WTO). Volatility in global oil and gas prices can significantly affect an economy. Falling prices can reduce incomes and disrupt economic stability. Tariff and non-tariff barriers, as well as instability in international trade, can affect economic growth.

Deepening regional cooperation enables the countries to establish common markets, improve transport links, and coordinate economic policies. Reducing dependence on individual markets by finding new trading partners and diversifying export markets.

Integration into the global economy requires not only participation in international organizations but also the implementation of strategies to improve trade relations and reduce trade barriers. This also includes adaptation to international standards and rules.

In a transition economy, the state's role changes from being the main owner formulating the dominant financial policy to one implementing the policy of prudential regulation, providing macroeconomic stability, balanced economic development, social sphere support, the rule of law, and the creation of conditions for the accelerated development of market relations. Many countries in the region have retained a high level of political centralization. This can slow down reforms and lead to political instability. Effective regulation requires a balance between market support and governmental intervention. It is important to establish clear boundaries for governmental intervention so as not to impede market mechanisms.

1.2.8 *Risks of economic instability*

Transition economies are often exposed to risks related to economic instability, such as inflation, currency crises, and sudden changes in government revenues and expenditures. Economic development can be extremely uneven, leading to economic and social disparities between different regions. Managing economic risks requires a comprehensive approach, including diversifying income sources and establishing reserve funds. This will help mitigate the effects of economic shocks and ensure more sustainable development.

1.2.9 *Social changes and financial stratification of society*

Transition economies often experience significant social changes, including rising unemployment, increasing social inequality, and declining living standards for some groups. This is due to the transition from a state-based system of employment and social guarantees to more market-based mechanisms. Internal and external migration flows affect the labor market and social structure, creating additional challenges for social policy. Rapid urban growth puts pressure on infrastructure, including housing, transport, and social services.

Development and implementation of social programs aimed at reducing inequality and improving social security. Social policy should include measures to support vulnerable groups, such as the unemployed and retired. One of the important areas is the formation of social security systems that will help mitigate the negative consequences of economic reforms.

1.3 Common Features and Key Differences Among the Economic Models of Central Asian Countries

The transition economies of Central Asia, including Kazakhstan, Uzbekistan, Kyrgyzstan, Tajikistan, and Turkmenistan, possess their own unique characteristics and challenges due to their historical, political, and economic contexts. All of these countries have gone through significant changes since the collapse of the Soviet Union in 1991, when they began the transition from centrally planned economies to various forms of market economies. A comparative analysis of the economies of Central Asia (Kazakhstan, Uzbekistan, Kyrgyzstan, Tajikistan, and Turkmenistan) reveals common features and key differences in their economic models, development strategies, and achievements. The main aspects for comparison are presented in the following sections.

1.3.1 *Economic structure and private sector development*

Kazakhstan has the most developed and diversified economy in the region. The oil and gas sector is the core, providing a significant portion of GDP and exports. The main macroeconomic indicators of Kazakhstan are presented in Table 1.3.

Kazakhstan is actively developing the private sector, especially through programs to support small- and medium-sized businesses. The country has attracted significant foreign investments, contributing to infrastructure and industrial development.

Table 1.3. Key macroeconomic indicators of Kazakhstan.

No.	Name of the Indicator	2000	2010	2020	2023	Growth (× times)
1.	Population, million people	14.9	16.4	18.9	19.4	1.3
2.	GDP, billion USD	18.3	148.1	169.8	220.0	9.3
3.	Inflation, % y/y	13.4	7.1	6.8	20.3	1.5
4.	Tenge to US dollar exchange rate	144.5	147.4	211.4	460.0	1.5
5.	Public debt, % of GDP	17.6	10.7	26.4	28.5	1.5
6.	Foreign trade goods turnover, billion dollars	19.2	76.9	97.5	122.0	5.1

Source: Developed by the author based on data from the National Statistical Committee of the Kazakh Republic, the National Bank of the Kazakh Republic, IMF, and CEIC.

Uzbekistan's economy is gradually diversifying, although for a long time the main income source remained agriculture and the export of natural resources such as cotton and natural gas. Since 2016, there has been an intensification of market reforms and the development of the private sector, including foreign investment attraction. The main macroeconomic indicators of Uzbekistan are presented in Table 1.4.

An economy with emphasis on agriculture, mining, and small business is typical of Kyrgyzstan. Privatization was carried out quickly, but the private sector remains weak. A significant portion of GDP is provided by remittances from labor migrants. The main macroeconomic indicators of Kyrgyzstan are presented in Table 1.5.

Tajikistan's economy is focused on agriculture, hydropower, and mining. The country has natural resources: gold, non-ferrous metals (primarily lead and zinc), and coal. In addition, Tajikistan has significant potential in the field of hydropower. This, in particular, made it possible in the 1970s to organize aluminum production based on imported raw materials at the Rogun hydroelectric power station, which still remains one of the country's key sources of export income.

The mineral processing industries, especially deep processing, have considerable potential for further development – currently, non-ferrous metals (except aluminum) are exported as ore concentrates and cotton as cotton fiber and yarn (not fabric). The private sector is developing slowly, and the state retains significant influence over key industries. As in Kyrgyzstan, remittances play an important role in the economy. The main macroeconomic indicators of Tajikistan are presented in Table 1.6.

Table 1.4. Key macroeconomic indicators of Uzbekistan.

No.	Name of the Indicator	2000	2010	2020	2023	Growth (× times)
1.	Population, million people	24.8	29.1	34.6	37.0	1.5
2.	GDP, billion USD	17.2	50.0	59.9	77.5	4.5
3.	Inflation, % y/y	25.0	7.5	12.9	10.0	1.3
4.	Soum to US dollar exchange rate	325	1,640	10,477	12,320	37.9
5.	Public debt, % of GDP	29.5	6.6	37.6	37.0	1.3
6.	Foreign trade goods turnover, billion dollars	6.2	22.2	37.6	48.0	7.7

Source: Developed by the author based on data from the State Statistics Committee of the Republic of Uzbekistan, the Central Bank of the Republic of Uzbekistan, and IMF.

Table 1.5. Key macroeconomic indicators of Kyrgyzstan.

No.	Name of the Indicator	2000	2010	2020	2023	Growth (× times)
1.	Population, million people	4.9	5.5	6.5	6.7	1.4
2.	GDP, billion USD	1.4	4.8	7.8	9.8	5.6
3.	Inflation, % y/y	20.9	8.0	9.7	12.0	1.5*
4.	Som to US dollar exchange rate	48.3	47.1	82.6	92.0	1.8
5.	Public debt, % of GDP	123.3	59.7	67.6	75.0	1.3*
6.	Foreign trade goods turnover, billion dollars	1.2	5.9	6.5	7.5	6.3

*Compared to 2010.

Source: Developed by the author based on data from the National Statistical Committee of the Kyrgyz Republic, the National Bank of the Kyrgyz Republic, IMF, and CEIC.

Table 1.6. Key macroeconomic indicators of Tajikistan.

No.	Name of the Indicator	2000	2010	2020	2023	Growth (× times)
1.	Population, million people	4.9	5.5	6.5	9.5	1.9
2.	GDP, billion USD	1.4	4.8	7.8	10.6	7.6
3.	Inflation, % y/y	20.9	8.0	9.7	8.7	1.1*
4.	Somoni to US dollar exchange rate	2.2	4.4	11.3	11.0	5
5.	Public debt, % of GDP	123.3	59.7	67.6	60.0	1.1
6.	Foreign trade goods turnover, billion dollars	1.2	5.9	6.5	8.5	7.1

*Compared to 2010.
Source: Developed by the author based on data from the Agency on Statistics under the President of the Republic of Tajikistan and the National Bank of Tajikistan.

Table 1.7. Key macroeconomic indicators of Turkmenistan.

No.	Name of the Indicator	2000	2010	2020	2023	Growth (× times)
1.	Population, million people	4.5	5.1	6.0	6.3	1.4
2.	GDP, billion USD	8.5	34.8	53.2	68.0	8.0
3.	Inflation, % y/y	8.0	4.4	10.0	13.5	1.7
4.	Manat to US dollar exchange rate	1.04	2.85	3.5	3.5	3.4
5.	Public debt, % of GDP	73.7	6.3	13.1	20.0	2.7
6.	Foreign trade goods turnover, billion dollars	3.7	7.4	11.2	14.0	3.8

*Compared to 2010.
Source: Developed by the author based on data from the World Bank, Asian Development Bank, IMF and Trade Map.

Turkmenistan remains the most closed country in the region. The economy remains highly centralized, and key sectors such as the gas industry remain under state control. The private sector is underdeveloped, and foreign investment is limited. The main macroeconomic indicators of Turkmenistan are presented in Table 1.7.

Turkmenistan's progress in improving the business environment and privatizing state-owned enterprises has been moderate since the early 1990s, limiting economic development outside the energy sector. High energy prices in the mid-2000s allowed the government to allocate large amounts of funds for development and social needs. Falling prices since mid-2014 have slowed Turkmenistan's economic growth and reduced government revenues.

1.3.2 *Level of economic diversification*

Economic diversification is critical for the sustainable development of Central Asian countries. Kazakhstan is actively trying to diversify its economy through the development of non-resource industries, such as agriculture, mechanical engineering, and information technology. The following are the key aspects of diversification:

- **Agriculture** – introduction of new technologies, irrigation, and crop selection improvements: The country aims to increase agricultural exports, including grain and meat, which will help increase foreign exchange earnings.

- **Machinery** – development of production capacities: This includes support for local producers, creation of joint ventures with foreign capital, and import substitution, involving the stimulation of equipment and machinery production for various industries, including agriculture and construction.
- **Information technologies** – economy digitalization: Active investments have been made in the IT sector and startups; technology parks and incubators have been established to support innovative projects.
- **Education** – training and advanced training of IT specialists to create a competitive workforce.

The country is implementing large-scale state programs to support non-oil exports – the Nurly Zhol and Business Roadmap programs are aimed at supporting non-oil exports by providing financial and tax incentives.

The economy diversification of Kazakhstan is a complex and multifaceted process that requires a comprehensive approach, including reforms in the areas of governance, education, infrastructure, and the financial system. Solving existing problems and forming a more favorable environment for business are key factors for the successful implementation of the diversification strategy.

Since gaining independence, Uzbekistan has been active in diversifying its economy. Reforms initiated by the country's leadership have allowed it to transform the economy from a predominantly agricultural to an industrial one. The share of industrial production in GDP increased from 9 to 27%. New industries were organized, including the automobile industry (in partnership with GM, Isuzu, and MAN), agricultural machinery (Case and Claas), and the electronic industry (Samsung and LG), as well as enterprises in the textile, pharmaceutical, light, and food industries. New oil and gas facilities were developed, and existing ones were modernized with the involvement of foreign investors (China National Petroleum Corporation (CNPC), Lukoil, Gazprom, Petronas, Total Energies, ExxonMobil, etc.), and transport machinery was re-established (Russian Railways, Transmashholding, Siemens Mobility, etc.).

Since 2016, Uzbekistan's economic diversification has received additional impetus thanks to the reforms initiated by the President Sh. M. Mirziyoyev. An important direction of these reforms was the opening of the market and the development of various sectors of the economy. Industrial production, tourism, and agriculture are actively developing, aimed at reducing the country's dependence on the export of natural resources. Key areas of economic diversification are as follows:

- **Industrial production** – establishment of special economic zones to attract investors and support local production, the introduction of modern production methods, and the development of high technologies.
- **Tourism** – investments in infrastructure, the development of hotels and transport sectors, improving services, attracting tourists through unique historical and cultural sites, gastronomic tourism, and ziyorat tourism.
- **Agriculture** – reforms in the agricultural sector, including reducing government control and supporting private initiatives.
- **Export opportunities** – increasing the production of quality products for export, including fruits and vegetables.

Despite its success, Uzbekistan faces challenges such as the heritage of a centralized economy, a lack of transparency, and complex bureaucratic procedures.

The economies of Kyrgyzstan and Tajikistan remain poorly diversified, with agriculture and mining being dominant. Both countries are working to develop hydropower, which could help diversification.

Political instability, corruption, and lack of investments limit the scope for deep structural changes in these countries. Both countries also face challenges related to a shortage of skilled labor and the need to reform the educational system.

The economy of Turkmenistan remains heavily dependent on natural gas exports. Efforts to diversify the economy are limited, and government efforts are focused on supporting the gas sector.

Economic diversification is crucial for sustainable development in Central Asia. Kazakhstan and Uzbekistan are taking active steps in this direction by attracting investment and implementing reforms. Kyrgyzstan and Tajikistan face serious challenges, but hydropower could be a key area for their growth. Turkmenistan, in turn, remains dependent on the gas sector, which limits its opportunities. Successful diversification requires continuing reforms aimed at developing non-resource sectors, creating a safe and predictable environment for investors, and improving the overall economic infrastructure.

1.3.3 *The role of foreign investment*

Foreign investment plays a key role in the economic development of Central Asia, providing the necessary capital for growth and modernization of various sectors. Let's take a closer look at the role of foreign investment in each Central Asian state, its impact on the country's economy, and the main challenges faced by investors.

Kazakhstan stands out as a key player in attracting foreign investment in Central Asia. The main investment areas are as follows:

- **Oil and gas sector:** Kazakhstan has large oil and gas reserves. Major international companies such as Chevron, ExxonMobil, and Total are actively involved in the development of deposits. Investments in this sector provide not only capital inflows but also the creation of jobs.
- **Infrastructure:** Investments in transport infrastructure, including roads, railways, and logistics centers, facilitate Kazakhstan's integration into international trade routes, especially within the framework of the Belt and Road Initiative.
- **Manufacturing industry:** Investments in this area aimed at diversifying the economy, creating competitive industries, and increasing export potential.

Kazakhstan also actively attracts foreign investment through the Astana International Financial Centre.

Despite the success, Kazakhstan faces challenges such as corruption and the need to improve the legal system and protect investors' rights.

Since 2016, Uzbekistan has stepped up its efforts to attract foreign investment. Key sectors for foreign investments include the following:

- **Textile industry:** Attracting investments in fabric and clothing production has become a priority as the country seeks to increase exports and create added value.
- **Construction:** Development of infrastructure, including residential and commercial buildings, also received significant funding.
- **Agriculture:** Investments are aimed at the modernization of the agricultural sector and the introduction of new technologies.

While the reforms have been successful, there is a need for greater legal transparency and a reduction of bureaucracy in the country.

In Kyrgyzstan, foreign investment is limited and concentrated in the mining sector (gold) and hydropower. Political instability reduces the country's attractiveness to investors.

In Tajikistan, foreign investment is mainly directed to hydropower and mining. As in Kyrgyzstan, political and economic instability are serious barriers to attracting investment. In addition, the lack of infrastructure and high risks for investors create barriers to attracting foreign investment.

Key areas for attracting foreign investment in Turkmenistan are as follows:

- **Gas sector:** The country is actively attracting investment in the development of gas fields, but these are mainly coming from a limited number of countries.
- **Industry:** Some attempts to diversify the economy toward processing industries are also being made. The main investments come from countries interested in the gas sector.

Overall, foreign investment plays a decisive role in the economic development of Central Asia, contributing to the modernization of infrastructure and the creation of jobs. However, the countries of the region face common challenges, such as political instability, corruption, and the need to improve the legal environment. To successfully attract investment, it is necessary to continue reforms aimed at forming a safer and more predictable environment for investors.

1.3.4 *Socio-economic development and living standards*

In Central Asia, socio-economic development and living standards vary greatly due to historical, political, and economic factors. Let us consider the situation in each country in more detail. The highest standard of living among the Central Asian countries, with a relatively high GDP per capita and developed social infrastructure, is achieved in Kazakhstan. The state actively invests in education, healthcare, and social programs.

Despite the success, Kazakhstan faces problems such as uneven development of regions and social inequality.

In recent years, the standard of living in Uzbekistan has improved significantly, especially in large cities. The state invests in social programs and infrastructure development. However, poverty remains high in rural areas, where the lack of jobs and limited access to education and health services are becoming serious problems. The state continues to develop strategies to reduce poverty and improve social security.

Kyrgyzstan and Tajikistan have the lowest living standards in the region. Both countries face high levels of poverty, unemployment, and migration. In Kyrgyzstan, more than 20% of the population live below the poverty line, while in Tajikistan this figure reaches 30%. Dependence on remittances from migrant workers working in Russia and other countries plays a critical role in supporting family incomes. This dependence makes the economy vulnerable to external factors, such as changes in migration policies or economic crises in destination countries.

Turkmenistan, despite significant social benefits such as free gas, water, and electricity, faces low living standards, especially outside major cities. The country's economy relies heavily on natural gas export revenues, making it vulnerable to fluctuations in world prices. In recent years, economic stagnation has led to a deterioration in social indicators such as access to healthcare and education. Government efforts to support the population often prove insufficient to address the accumulated issues, especially in remote areas.

Each country in Central Asia faces unique challenges and opportunities. Kazakhstan continues to lead in living standards, while Uzbekistan has made steps to improve the situation but still struggles with rural poverty. Kyrgyzstan and Tajikistan need systematic reforms to improve living standards, and Turkmenistan faces economic difficulties despite significant social guarantees.

Comprehensive measures are necessary to improve the economic situation and social infrastructure and to reduce inequality for the sustainable development of the region in the future.

1.3.5 *Political stability and impact on the economy*

A relatively stable political situation in Kazakhstan contributes to economic development, although there are risks related to power concentration and the lack of political competition.

Political stability in Uzbekistan has increased since the change of power in 2016, which has had a positive impact on the economy. Reforms aimed at improving the business climate and social stability are ongoing.

Frequent changes of power and political instability in the Kyrgyz Republic have a negative impact on the economy, creating obstacles to long-term planning and development.

The political situation in Tajikistan is stable, but there are barriers to economic development and investment attraction.

Turkmenistan maintains stability by following a centralized economic model but lags behind in implementing large-scale reforms and openness to international economic integration.

The economies of Central Asian countries demonstrate significant diversity in their approaches to reform and the results of the transition from a planned to a market economy. Kazakhstan leads the region in terms of economic development, diversification, and investment attraction, while Uzbekistan has recently demonstrated a high pace of economic reforms. Kyrgyzstan and Tajikistan face serious social and economic problems, including poverty and political instability. Turkmenistan maintains a centralized economic model, remaining one of the most closed countries in the world. In general, the success of economic reforms and stable development depends on a number of factors, including political stability, the effectiveness of state institutions, the level of corruption, and the ability to diversify the economy.

The formation of a domestic financial sector, an important part of which is the insurance market, is an essential condition for the sustainable development of the countries in the region. The main tasks are to overcome the population's mistrust and to diversify the development of financial services. The initial period of rapid development and expansion of credit activity, based on foreign capital and inflows of export revenues, helped to attract a wide range of companies and households in the financial market. However, depositors and investors do not trust the financial sector enough. The population prefers "traditional" methods of protecting against risks and savings, not trusting insurance policies and deposits. In emergency situations, the population relies more on material assistance from family and friends than on insurance and loans from banks. In addition, although the network of financial institutions in the regions is expanding, access to them in remote areas remains insufficient. The low degree of inclusiveness of the financial system can contribute to the persistence of income inequality among the population, slowing down the development of human capital due to limited access to education and health services.

Political stability, the effectiveness of state institutions, corruption level, and the ability of countries to diversify the economy are all critical factors for the success of economic reforms in Central Asia. To achieve sustainable development, it is necessary to work on improving the political situation, providing legal guarantees for business, and creating conditions for long-term investment. The future of the region will depend on the ability of states to adapt to new challenges, develop open and inclusive economic models, and build partnerships in the international arena.

1.4 Conclusions

1. The analysis of studies of transition economies in the Central Asian countries exposes the multidimensional and complex nature of the post-Soviet transformation processes. It has been determined that economic reforms in the region were carried out in the context of institutional immaturity, a weak legal framework, and high dependence on the export of natural resources. Theoretically, the discourse is focused on shock therapy models, gradual reforms, and institutional changes; moreover, empirical works emphasize financial stabilization, the state's role, and integration into the global economy. The studies demonstrate a variety of approaches but have a limited consideration of the local context and socio-cultural determinants. Despite progress in certain sectors, the sustainability and depth of transformation remain limited, requiring further interdisciplinary analysis and institutional understanding of transition processes.
2. The economic systems of the Central Asian countries represent comprehensive transition models formed under the influence of historical, cultural, geopolitical, and natural resource factors. Despite significant progress, expressed in sustainable GDP growth, investment growth, and foreign trade activity, the region continues to face systemic challenges related to institutional immaturity, a weak law enforcement environment, limited access to global markets, and socio-economic fragmentation. The specifics of the transition economy have emerged in the necessity for simultaneous reform of the legal, financial, and market infrastructure, as well as in the production structure diversification. The sustainability of further development of the countries in the region directly depends on the state policy's effectiveness in the field of legal modernization, institution building, social support, and integration into the global economic space.
3. The economic models of the Central Asian countries are characterized by both the presence of common features inherited from the planned Soviet system and significant differences due to political course, economic structure, and openness level. Kazakhstan demonstrates the highest degree of market transformation, economic diversification, and institutional sustainability. Kyrgyzstan and Tajikistan remain vulnerable due to a weak institutional base, low diversification, and dependence on labor migration. Turkmenistan maintains a centralized model with limited access to external investment and minimal diversification. Uzbekistan, with its status as the largest economy in Central Asia and demonstrating sustainable macroeconomic dynamics, is a representative case for analyzing transformation processes in developing countries. Active public administration reform, investment climate, and the digitalization of economic institutions, including in the insurance sector, determine its research significance. Despite the presence of structural limitations – such as a low level of insurance culture and vulnerability to natural risks – the country is developing the potential for the introduction of advanced technologies, including artificial intelligence, which makes it a strategically important platform for the approbation of solutions in the field of ESG insurance transformation.

Chapter 2

ESG Transformation of the Insurance Business in Countries with Transition Economies

2.1 Economic Essence and Goals of ESG Transformation of the Insurance Business

In Uzbekistan, as well as throughout the world, the concept of ESG transformation of the insurance business is becoming increasingly important. The concepts of sustainable development and ESG transformation have evolved from simple ideas into interconnected, complex global instruments aimed at preserving the Earth's ecosystems while achieving high rates of economic growth. The concept of sustainable development is based on the idea of meeting the needs of the present generation without damaging the needs of future generations. ESG is based on the principles of sustainable development and serves as a metric that allows us to assess how "sustainably" an insurance company operates. The uniqueness of the ESG transformation phenomenon lies in its principles, according to which the sustainable development of an insurer goes beyond environmental issues; when managing an insurance company, it is also necessary to take into account social and corporate factors.

In the insurance industry, the "business-as-usual" approach is gradually giving way to a new approach in which the success of an insurance company is measured not only by financial indicators but also by its positive impact on society and environmental sustainability. The economic essence of the ESG transformation of an insurance business is the systematic integration of the principles of environmental, social, and corporate responsibility into the strategy and operational processes of the company. This transformation changes both the internal and external aspects of the insurance company's functioning, which ultimately affects its financial stability, competitiveness, and long-term profitability. This transformation is aimed at creating long-term sustainability, increasing trust from customers and investors, and improving reputation in the market.

ESG transformation of the insurance business is not just compliance with fashion trends or regulatory requirements. This is a deep economic transformation aimed at creating sustainable and responsible businesses capable of adapting to changes and ensuring long-term profitability in conditions of growing challenges to the transforming economy. The ESG transformation of the insurance business is the process of adaptation of insurance companies to the modern requirements of sustainable development. The concept of ESG transformation in the insurance business is becoming especially relevant both in Uzbekistan and around the world. Sustainable development and ESG principles are integrated into the strategic and operational processes of professional participants in the insurance market, allowing them to not only meet modern requirements but also create a positive impact on society and the environment.

The economic essence of ESG transformation of the insurance business is characterized by the following principles:

- Environmental responsibility includes measures to reduce the company's ecological footprint, for example, through energy efficiency, reducing carbon emissions, and waste and resource management. In the insurance business, this may be expressed in identifying and assessing climate risks, investing in "green" assets, and developing insurance products that support environmentally friendly technologies, and refusing to insure risks from "brown" production.
- Social responsibility includes a responsible approach to the management of the labor force of the insurance market, ensuring fair and safe working conditions, supporting gender diversity and inclusion, and participating in social initiatives aimed at improving the quality of life. In addition, in the insurance business, these principles include the introduction of insurance products protecting socially vulnerable groups, supporting education and health, as well as the charitable activities of insurers.
- Corporate liability of insurers includes practices of effective management, transparency, reporting, and compliance with high ethical standards of conducting the insurance business.

Compliance with the above-mentioned principles by professional participants in the insurance market is important in maintaining investor and client confidence, minimizing the risks of corruption and conflicts of interest. ESG transformation allows insurers to more effectively manage risks related to climate change, social unrest, and compliance risks.

For example, insurance companies integrating ESG principles can more accurately assess and manage risks from natural disasters and emergency situations or social inequality, reducing losses and increasing resilience to crises. Increasingly, external and internal investors are targeting insurance companies with high ESG scores. Such companies attract investment on more favorable terms, as they are seen as less risky and more sustainable in the long term. Key aspects of the economic essence of the insurance business's ESG transformation are presented in Fig. 2.1. Let us consider them in more detail.

Sustainable insurance is an important tool in the context of climate change and sustainable development. Sustainable insurance involves developing new policies that take into account the risks related to climate change and environmental factors.

Sustainable insurance not only helps protect customers from climate risks but also offers insurance coverage for companies using renewable energy sources such as solar or wind turbines, and insures "green" vehicles such as electric cars at lower rates for owners.

In addition, sustainable insurance involves the implementation of modern risk management technologies, allowing clients to minimize potential losses, as well as using digitalization for more accurate calculation of insurance rates and individualization of policies. Insurance companies implementing ESG principles form ecosystems around themselves and can offer their clients unique products, meeting the new requirements and expectations of society.

Thus, sustainable insurance is becoming an integral part of insurance companies' strategies during the conditions of climate change. This approach helps protect clients from environmental risks and contributes to building more sustainable and responsible businesses. Integrating ESG principles into insurance opens up new opportunities for development and strengthens trust among clients, investors, and society as a whole.

Sustainable investments are becoming an important component of the modern financial world, especially in the context of fighting climate change and social challenges.

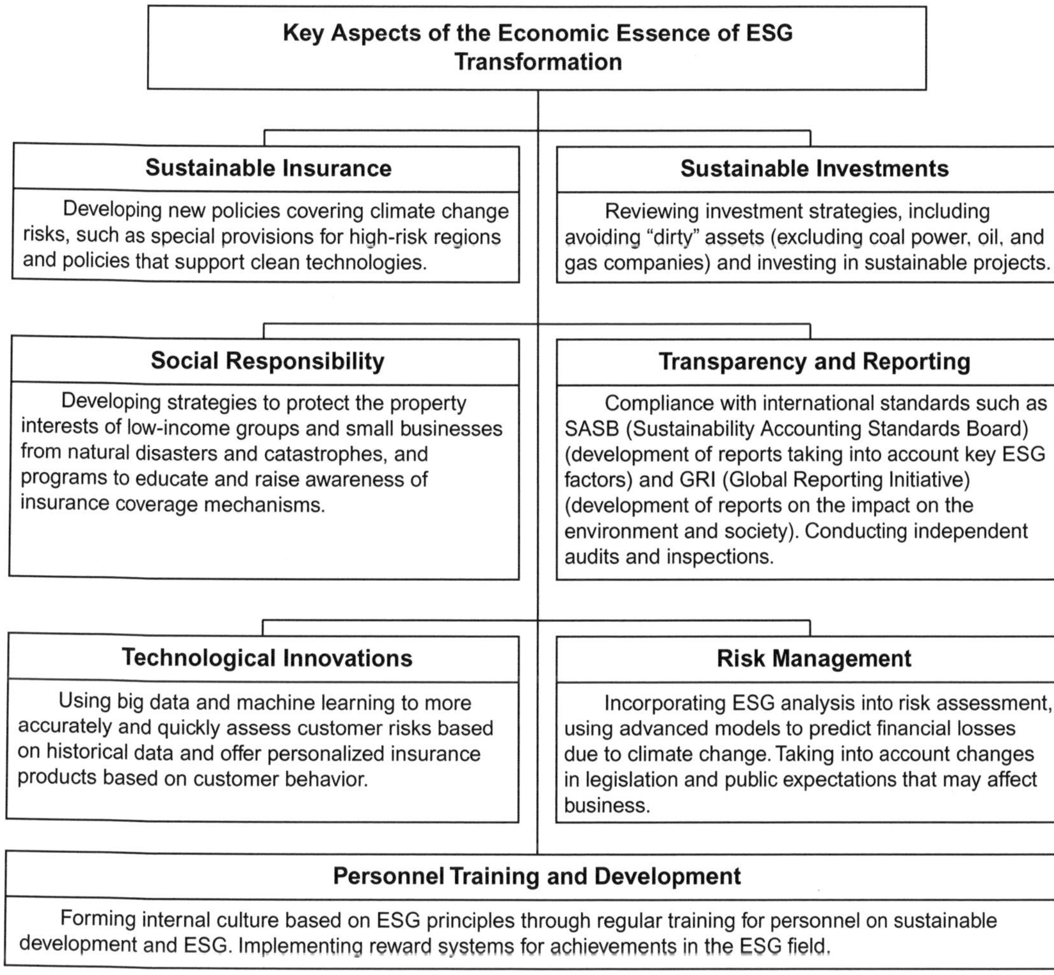

Fig. 2.1. Key aspects of the economic essence of the insurance business's ESG transformation.

This includes revising investment strategies to exclude "dirty" assets (coal power plants, oil and gas companies, etc.) and supporting sustainable projects. This aspect of the economic essence of the insurance business's ESG transformation takes into account not only financial efficiency but also the social impact of insurance companies when carrying out their investment activities. This includes avoiding investments in companies with poor working conditions, human rights violations, or environmental crimes.

Increasing the share of green bonds in insurers' investment portfolios allows funds to be directed toward projects that bring environmental benefits, such as the development of renewable energy sources, improved energy efficiency, and sustainable resource management.

Investing insurers' temporarily available funds into sustainable infrastructure, including public transport, smart cities, water management systems, and sustainable housing projects, not only promotes economic growth but also helps adapt to climate change.

Sustainable investing is a strategic approach to capital investment that not only generates financial returns but also responds to the challenges of the modern world. Rethinking investment strategies with an emphasis on eliminating "dirty" assets and supporting sustainable projects creates new opportunities for growth and development for both businesses and society as a whole. Implementing ESG principles and transparency in reporting strengthens investor confidence and contributes to the formation of a more sustainable and responsible financial sector.

The social responsibility of the insurance business includes the development of strategies aimed at protecting the property interests of low-income groups of the population and small businesses. These strategies are aimed not only at providing insurance protection but also at creating a more resilient and informed society capable of coping with the challenges related to risks and disasters.

Following such international standards as SASB and GRI, as well as conducting independent audits and reviews, helps to increase the transparency and reporting of insurance companies. Insurers should not only consider ESG factors in their reports but also integrate them into their strategy. This may include changes in management, operations, and even corporate culture. For example, insurance companies can integrate sustainability principles into decision-making and in the assessment of executive performance.

These measures not only build trust among interested parties but also help insurance companies effectively manage their social and environmental risks. Creating a system of transparency and responsibility is a key element in achieving sustainable development and social responsibility of insurance market professional participants. GRI reports allow insurance companies to demonstrate their achievements in the field of sustainable development, as well as identify areas for improvement.

Technological innovations such as big data, machine learning, and blockchain are transforming the insurance industry by providing more accurate risk assessment, personalized offers, and increased transparency. These technologies not only improve the customer experience but also help insurers manage risk more effectively and minimize fraud. However, successful integration of these technologies requires taking into account challenges related to data privacy, information quality and regulatory aspects.

Risk management in the modern insurance business requires a comprehensive approach that includes integrating ESG analysis into risk assessment, using advanced models to predict climate-related losses, taking into account changes in legislation and public expectations, and developing adaptive response plans. These measures help insurers not only reduce potential financial losses but also increase the company's resilience and improve its reputation and trust with stakeholders. In the environment of uncertainty and constant change, such an approach is a key to achieving long-term success.

Forming an internal culture based on ESG principles requires the insurer to take a systematic approach, including regular personnel training and effective reward system implementation. This not only helps to increase awareness and personnel involvement in sustainable development but also strengthens the company's reputation, improves its sustainability, and creates competitive advantages. Ultimately, such a culture contributes to the achievement of the company's strategic goals and responds to the challenges of the modern world.

In modern insurance, customers are increasingly paying attention to the social and environmental responsibility of insurance companies. Insurers that demonstrate a commitment to ESG principles can count on increased trust from insureds and investors. This trust leads to greater loyalty, which in turn contributes to the growth of the customer base and an increase in investment volume.

In addition, ESG transformation helps insurance companies improve their reputation in the market, especially among the younger generation of potential insureds and investors who value social responsibility and sustainability.

Motivating customers to adopt sustainable practices such as energy-efficient technologies or recycling and waste reduction can result in significant reductions in operating costs for both the insurer and the insured.

The ESG transformation of the insurance business promotes the development of innovative products and services that meet new challenges and opportunities. This applies primarily to insurance services related to protection against climate change risks, which support sustainable development and social justice.

Fig. 2.2. Key goals of ESG transformation.

Companies that successfully integrate ESG principles can expect stable revenue and growth in profits over the long term. This is due to better risk management, loyal customers and investors, and a reduction in operating costs.

The goals of ESG transformation of the insurance business cover a wide range of aspects related to sustainability, social responsibility, and effective corporate governance. These goals reflect the desire of insurance companies not only to improve their economic efficiency but also to contribute to solving global problems such as climate change, social inequality, and supporting sustainable development. The key goals of ESG transformation of the insurance business are presented in Fig. 2.2.

Let us consider the above-mentioned aspects in more detail. The meaning of the "Reducing the Carbon Footprint" goal is minimizing an insurance company's negative impact on the environment. This may include reducing carbon emissions, reducing energy and water consumption, reducing waste, using renewable energy sources, and improving energy efficiency in offices and data centers. In addition, insurers should encourage insureds and potential clients to reduce their carbon footprint and, where possible, avoid investing in "brown" objects.

The "Climate Risk Management" goal means that insurers are making efforts to better understand and manage climate-related risks, such as natural disasters and emergent situations, that could impact their financial resilience. This could include developing new insurance products that address climate risks, as well as integrating climate factors into the investment decisions of the insureds and insurers.

The "Support for Sustainable Projects" goal is achieved by the development and promotion of "green" insurance products that support environmentally friendly technologies and practices. In addition, insurers can actively invest in projects that promote sustainable development, such as renewable energy, sustainable agriculture, and climate-resilient infrastructure.

One of the ESG transformations of the insurance business is to contribute to the creation of a more inclusive and fair society. Insurance companies should develop inclusive products and services aimed at socially vulnerable groups, such as low-income groups, people with disabilities, retired residents of remote areas, and private and small businesses with insufficient working capital. It is also important to ensure equal career opportunities and working conditions for all employees, regardless of gender, race, age, or other characteristics.

In implementing the "Social Responsibility and Participation in Local Communities" aspect, insurance companies should actively participate in the life of local communities, supporting social initiatives such as charity, volunteer programs, and projects aimed at improving education and healthcare. This helps to strengthen social stability and increase trust in the company.

The ESG transformation of the insurance business involves creating safe and fair working conditions for all employees of the insurance organization and facilitating the creation of such conditions for personnel of the insured entities. This includes providing competitive wages, ensuring equal opportunities for career growth, protecting the employees' rights, and creating conditions for work-life balance.

To achieve the "Improving Corporate Governance" goal, insurance companies must improve their corporate governance systems and ensure transparency, reporting, and adherence to high ethical standards. This includes establishing effective management bodies, ensuring the independence of the board of directors, and implementing control and audit mechanisms to prevent corruption, fraud, and conflicts of interest.

As part of the ESG transformation, insurers are required to comply with all applicable laws and regulations, including those related to customer protection, sustainability, and environmental protection. This helps to avoid legal risks and strengthen the company's reputation.

Since the insurance business is based on trust, achieving the "Business Ethics and Responsibility" goal involves conducting business in accordance with high ethical standards. This includes following the principles of honesty, transparency, and responsibility to shareholders and society, as well as the implementation of codes of conduct for employees and partners.

ESG transformation encourages insurance companies to develop innovative products that respond to the current challenges. These could include, for example, insurance products covering risks related to climate change, health and well-being of the population, as well as products aimed at supporting small businesses and sustainable agriculture.

ESG transformation of the insurance business is impossible without a significant increase in the digitalization level of the insurer's work processes and the digital transformation of the insurance market as a whole, which improves interaction with clients and makes insurance services more accessible and transparent. The introduction of digital platforms for online sales, remote policy management, and claims processing can significantly improve the quality of customer service and reduce the insurer's operating costs.

The implementation of innovation in insurance is usually a long-term process requiring funding (sometimes significant) and has a high degree of uncertainty, so the issues of professional compliance of insurer employees are of particular importance. The unsatisfied demand for qualified specialists with skills and competencies related to solving high-tech problems (IT specialists, programmers), specialists with skills in using modern gadgets and computer equipment, and employees of insurance companies with the appropriate qualifications, ready to work in the conditions of the modern digital environment, can lead to a significant lag in the ESG transformation of the domestic insurance market.

In the long term, the ESG transformation of the insurance business helps reduce costs, increase profits, and grow investment:

- First of all, a review of the insurer's activities by the ESG methodology allows us to evaluate the business processes' efficiency, rethink the values of the organization, and, thus, determine strategic directions for growth.

- Secondly, following ESG standards increases sustainability to non-financial risks, such as the climate change effects, the emergence of new technologies, or global pandemics. This is because in-time analysis of potential risks gives more time to develop strategies for adaptation to new conditions.
- ESG also opens up new opportunities for insurers' marketing and helps to raise the relationship between the insurance company and the insured to a new level. Addressing environmental, social, and governance issues can be used to position the insurer as a responsible business and attract new customers.
- Finally, the ESG implementation enhances the business reputation of the insurance company and allows it to attract highly qualified employees, who increasingly pay attention to the values and corporate culture of the employer when choosing a workplace.

2.2 Regional Peculiarities of ESG Transformation Regulation in Insurance

The specifics of ESG transformation regulation in insurance vary significantly depending on the country and region. These differences are due to legal, economic, cultural, and political factors that influence the implementation and practice of ESG principles in the insurance industry.

The European Union has a number of directives and regulations aimed at strengthening ESG obligations in the financial sector, including insurance. For example, the Sustainable Finance Disclosure Regulation (SFDR) and the EU Taxonomy Regulation require insurance companies to disclose information about their ESG risks and investments. The main objective of the SFDR is to enable investors operating in the European Economic Area to raise funds in a sustainable manner. By disclosing information about the environmental, social, and governance (ESG) aspects of financial instruments to investors in an easy-to-understand manner, the SFDR aims to increase transparency and reporting and prevent "greenwashing" (i.e. seeming environmental initiatives that are not accompanied by real actions or activities). After ESG principles became one of the factors for attracting financing, the practice of misleading stakeholders about the implementation of their environmental or social mission (the so-called "impact washing") has become widespread.

The EU Taxonomy determines whether a company's economic activity is sustainable based on six environmental objectives and four compliance requirements. The EU Taxonomy only provides classification and disclosure obligations and does not prohibit investment in an economic activity that does not meet the criteria. However, financing an economic activity that is considered unsustainable is deemed unfavorable in terms of conditions.

The main differences between the EU taxonomy and the SFDR are summarized in Table 2.1. European supervisors such as EIOPA actively monitor that insurers take into account ESG risks such as climate change when assessing their liabilities and forming reserves.[1]

In the EU, much attention is paid to the issues of social responsibility, equality, and good governance. This is reflected in requirements for disclosure of information on board diversity and anti-discrimination policies. Regulating ESG transformation of insurance is

[1] https://european-union.europa.eu/institutions-law-budget/institutions-and-bodies/search-all-eu-institutions-and-bodies/european-insurance-and-occupational-pensions-authority-eiopa_en.

Table 2.1. Comparison of SFDR and EU taxonomy.

	SFDR	EU Taxonomy
Application area	Basically, investment products (e.g. investment funds)	Mainly business and business activity
Target	Formulate investment products' sustainability from the ecological, social sphere, and management (ESG) point of view	Classify sustainable economic activities and identify the environmentally friendly activities of companies
Tasks	Information disclosure about ESG risks and investment products' classification	Presentation of a classification system for sustainable economic activity and assessment of companies' compliance with the criteria
Advantage	Easy for investors to compare different products	Companies are open in declaring their sustainability and increasing their credibility in the marketplace

Table 2.2. Key ESG initiatives in the states and provinces of North America.

State/Province	Key ESG Initiatives	Approximate Requirements
California	Climate risk reporting	Climate risk reporting principles
New York	Investment decision transparency	ESG factor disclosure
Massachusetts	Social responsibility of companies	Diversification and inclusion initiatives
Ontario	Supporting sustainable investment	Standards for green investments
British Columbia	Sustainable resource management	Environmental risk assessment programs

not only a challenge but also an opportunity to create a more sustainable and responsible business environment. Companies that are able to adapt to the new conditions will have a competitive advantage in the global market.

The EU approach to ESG regulation in insurance is therefore multilayered and systemic. It combines transparency requirements, supervision of compliance with standards, and attention to social responsibility. This creates conditions for the sustainable development of not only insurance companies but also the entire financial sector, which can serve as an example for other regions seeking a similar transformation.

In the US and Canada, ESG regulation in insurance varies from state to state and province to province. Some US states (such as California) have strict requirements for climate risk consideration, while other regions have less developed requirements.

In the US, large institutional investors such as pension funds play an important role, actively requiring insurance companies to consider ESG factors in their investment strategies.

In North America, civil society organizations and shareholders play a significant role in promoting ESG initiatives, putting pressure on insurers to be more transparent and accountable. The main ESG initiatives in the states and provinces of North America are listed in Table 2.2.

Table 2.3. Key ESG initiatives in the Asia-Pacific region.

Country	Key Initiatives	Notes
Japan	• TCFD (climate risks disclosure)	Active ESG implementation in business strategies
	• Tokyo Declaration	Corporate responsibility support
Australia	• Mandatory reports for large companies	ASIC support
	• Transparency programs	Sustainable investments
Singapore	• MAS Sustainable Finance Initiatives	ESG leader in the region
	• Sustainable Investment Platforms	Supporting companies with positive impact
South Korea	• Green Finance Act	Stimulating environmentally friendly technologies
	• Corporate ESG initiatives	Large companies' participation
China	• Regulations on ESG data disclosure	Green bond development
	• Reporting standards	Focus on environmentally sustainable projects
Malaysia	• ESG Reporting Guide	Corporate Social Responsibility Programs
	• Regulator support	Focus on local communities
Taiwan	• Mandatory ESG reports for public companies	Sustainable practices of large companies
	• State programs	Green economy support

The regulation of ESG transformation of insurance in the US and Canada is a complex and multifaceted process in which insurers face different requirements and expectations. Regional differences in approaches, institutional investor pressure, and the active position of civil society organizations create both challenges and opportunities for the implementation of sustainable practices.

Insurers that are prepared to adapt to these changes and effectively integrate ESG principles into their strategy will not only be able to enhance their reputation but also ensure long-term financial stability while responding to the challenges of the modern world.

In the Asia-Pacific region, ESG regulations of the insurance business vary greatly. The main ESG initiatives in the Asia-Pacific countries are summarized in Table 2.3.

Japan and Australia have seen a strong push for ESG principles in the financial sector, with a range of legislative initiatives and voluntary standards in place to encourage companies to take a more responsible approach to business.

Singapore has become one of the ESG leaders in the region, thanks to proactive efforts by the government and financial regulators. The Monetary Authority of Singapore (MAS) implements sustainable finance initiatives, including mandatory climate risk disclosures for financial institutions. The Singapore Exchange actively promotes sustainable investing, providing platforms for companies looking to raise funding for projects with a positive environmental impact.

South Korea has also been active in the ESG arena as reflected in its national sustainability strategy. In 2020, South Korea adopted a Green Finance Act that promotes investment in cleantech and sustainable development. Large companies such as Samsung and LG implement ESG principles into their strategies and reporting, which is confirmed by the international sustainability ratings.

China is actively working to integrate ESG into its economy, especially relating to sustainable development and climate change. The Chinese government has introduced regulations requiring companies to disclose ESG data and has also developed its own reporting standards. Green bonds, which finance environmentally sustainable projects, are actively being developed in China, which also stimulates demand for ESG investments.

Malaysia pays attention to integrating ESG principles into its financial and corporate practices. The Securities Commission Malaysia has developed guidelines for ESG reporting for companies. Malaysian companies are increasingly implementing corporate social responsibility programs focused on local communities and ecosystems.

Taiwan is also actively pursuing ESG initiatives, including mandatory reporting requirements for public companies. Taiwanese companies such as TSMC are actively implementing sustainable practices, including carbon reduction and resource management. The Taiwanese government supports green economy development through various programs and initiatives.

Thus, countries in the Asia-Pacific region continue to develop and adapt ESG principles to suit local conditions and needs. These efforts not only contribute to improving corporate responsibility but also form more resilient economies in the face of global challenges such as climate change and social change.

In Latin America, ESG regulations are in the early development stages, although some countries, such as Brazil and Chile, are beginning to actively implement ESG principles in the insurance sector.

The region pays great attention to social issues such as fighting poverty and inequality. These aspects are becoming an important part of ESG initiatives in insurance.

Economic instability in some countries in the region makes it difficult to implement ESG principles, as companies often focus on short-term profits rather than long-term sustainability.

In Africa, ESG regulations in insurance have been slow to develop, although some countries, such as South Africa, have begun to implement ESG standards, particularly in the areas of disclosure and sustainable investing.

In African countries, ESG principles often focus on social issues such as access to insurance for vulnerable groups.

The lack of infrastructure and resources in some African countries makes it difficult to implement ESG principles, especially in the context of environmental initiatives.

ESG regulation in insurance continues to evolve, and regional differences play a key role in determining how these principles are implemented in different parts of the world. The widespread adoption of ESG reporting allows governments to receive a more complete picture of how businesses are contributing to the SDGs. When there is a common framework and metrics that are understood by both the public and private sectors, financing for sustainable development becomes more effective, as governments can direct funds to areas where they are most needed.

In Central Asia, the specifics of the regulation of ESG transformation of insurance also have their own unique features, determined by the socioeconomic development, legal framework, and cultural characteristics of the region. Let us consider the key aspects of ESG transformation of the insurance industry in this region.

In Central Asia (Kazakhstan, Uzbekistan, Kyrgyzstan, Tajikistan, and Turkmenistan), the legal framework for ESG regulation in insurance is at an early stage. In some countries, the processes of developing and implementing standards related to sustainable development and socially responsible investment are at the initial stages.

Kazakhstan is a leader in the region in implementing sustainable development principles, which is partly reflected in the insurance industry. Government initiatives to develop a "green" economy and integrate ESG principles into the financial sector are actively promoted.

Insurers in Central Asia are starting to pay attention to climate risks, especially in the context of agriculture and water resources, which are critical for the region. Countries in the region often face droughts, floods, and other natural disasters, making it increasingly important to consider these risks.

Initiatives are emerging in Kazakhstan to develop "green" insurance, aimed at supporting environmentally friendly projects and the use of renewable energy sources.

In Central Asia, the ESG social component includes providing access to insurance products for the population, including rural and sparsely populated areas. In some countries in the region, such as Uzbekistan, there are attempts to improve access to insurance through digitalization and the promotion of microinsurance.

An important aspect of social regulation in the region is corporate social responsibility (CSR). However, unlike Western countries, where CSR has already been widely implemented, in Central Asia, these initiatives have only just begun to develop.

Governance and transparency issues are not yet at the forefront of the Central Asian insurance sector. However, international organizations and financial institutions operating in the region promote best corporate governance practices, including fighting corruption and increasing transparency.

In Kazakhstan, government agencies are actively involved in the formation and promotion of ESG principles, especially within the framework of international projects and cooperation with international financial institutions.

International financial institutions such as the World Bank, the International Finance Corporation (IFC), and the European Bank for Reconstruction and Development (EBRD) play an important role in promoting ESG principles in the insurance industry in Central Asia. These institutions support projects aimed at developing sustainable finance and ESG initiatives in the region (Table 2.4).

Global ESG trends such as sustainable development and responsible investing gradually penetrated Central Asia, influencing local insurance companies and regulators.

In Kyrgyzstan and Tajikistan, weak infrastructure and economic instability have made it difficult to implement ESG principles. However, growing interest in foreign investment and global markets integration has contributed to the gradual development of ESG initiatives.

Table 2.4. The role of international organizations in supporting ESG transformations in Central Asia.

Organization	Key Initiatives	Impact on the Region
World Bank	Financing sustainable projects	Green insurance support
IFC (International Finance Corporation)	Investments in environmentally friendly projects	Promoting Sustainable Investing
EBRD (European Bank for Reconstruction and Development)	Modernization and sustainable development projects	Development of ESG infrastructure and standards

Overall, ESG regulation of insurance in Central Asia is just beginning to take shape, and this process can be expected to intensify in the coming years, especially under the influence of international standards and global trends.

Uzbekistan has also seen growing interest in ESG aspects in the context of overall economic modernization strategies. Adaptation to regulatory changes is key, as different countries have different requirements for ESG standards compliance. Regulatory issues relating to ESG transformation of domestic insurance are becoming increasingly relevant as global sustainability standards are integrated into national economies.

The introduction of ESG principles into the insurance industry requires adaptation of the existing regulatory acts and development of new standards and methods. The main standards in the ESG sphere are as follows:

- The Global Reporting Initiative (GRI) Standard is a set of guidelines and standards for non-financial reporting by companies. This standard was developed to encourage organizations to disclose information about their sustainability and social responsibility. GRI is the most widely used standard for non-financial reporting.
- The Sustainability Accounting Standards Board (SASB) Standard focuses on specific industries and sustainability-related risk factors. This standard helps companies identify key sustainability factors relevant to their industry and incorporates them into their reporting.
- The Task Force on Climate-related Financial Disclosures (TCFD) Standard is related to climate risks and opportunities. It helps companies assess and disclose financial, operational, and strategic aspects related to climate change.
- The Carbon Disclosure Project (CDP) Standard provides a system for reporting greenhouse gas emissions and climate risk management. Companies can voluntarily disclose their climate data through the CDP, allowing investors and stakeholders to assess their climate strategy and performance.
- The ISSB (International Sustainability Standards Board) Standard is an international standard that brings together various sustainability standards, such as the GRI (Global Reporting Initiative). The ISSB develops common international standards for sustainability reporting, including ESG factors. It aims to create a unified and transparent framework that will help companies better understand and report on their sustainability, as well as facilitate the data comparison and companies' sustainability assessment at the international level.

Let us consider the key regulatory aspects related to the ESG transformation of the insurance industry.

The most important task is to develop a regulatory framework governing the reporting of ESG factors in insurance activities. This could include mandatory disclosure requirements on companies' climate risks, social impacts, and governance practices.

Current insurance regulations should be reviewed and adapted to take into account ESG aspects. For example, reporting and disclosure laws could be supplemented with provisions to disclose ESG data.

At the current stage of the domestic insurance market development, we consider it appropriate to introduce mandatory requirements for disclosure of information related to ESG factors by insurance companies. First of all, this should relate to data on the company's impact on the environment, social responsibility, and corporate governance practices. The introduction of uniform ESG reporting standards will help to unify the approaches of insurance companies to information disclosure and will facilitate data analysis for regulators and investors.

For successful ESG transformation of domestic insurance, it is important to implement and adapt international standards, such as the recommendations of the Task Force on Climate-related Financial Disclosures (TCFD) or the principles of sustainable insurance (PSI) from the UN Environment Programme.

Today, there are over 70 standards (meaning only one thing – there is no ESG standard) and about 600 rating systems that are used to assess companies: They characterize the quality of their corporate governance, commitment to the "green" economy, or the workforce diversity values. However, none of them are comprehensive and all-encompassing. ISO Standards (14000, 26000, etc.) are widely known; they are characterized by global recognition in all industries, they lack a perceptible basis for assessing compliance (e.g. a list of criteria), and have limited disclosure potential.

The Carbon Disclosure Project standards are also used by the largest corporations around the world and are distinguished due to their ease of use. However, the emphasis on environmental indicators (such as carbon footprint, water and energy consumption) and the focus on the largest companies (e.g. FT Global 500) for public disclosure significantly limit its application scope.

Global Reporting Initiative standards take a special position and are characterized by global recognition, widespread application in different countries and industries, ease of use, availability of templates, and constant updating. However, the flexible choice of criteria leads to overestimation or underestimation of indicators reporting. In addition, the standard is open to subjective and biased assessments.

In the near future, we consider it appropriate for the Association of Professional Participants of the Insurance Market of Uzbekistan and the National Agency for Perspective Projects of the Republic of Uzbekistan to develop recommendations on the methodology for assessing ESG risks, including climate risks that may affect the financial stability of insurance organizations in the republic. This is especially relevant for insurance companies that have assets exposed to climate or environmental risks.

It is also relevant to conduct stress tests taking into account ESG risks, which will allow insurance companies to better prepare for possible adverse scenarios related to climate change, social unrest, or changes in corporate governance.

An important step in regulating the ESG transformation of the insurance business may be the introduction of regulations stimulating responsible investments by domestic insurers. In this case, insurers will have to take into account ESG factors when making investment decisions in order to reduce risks and increase portfolio sustainability.

In order to stimulate the development and implementation of insurance products aimed at sustainable development (for example, "green" projects insurance), we consider it appropriate to provide tax breaks or other incentives for such initiatives.

Setting standards for corporate governance in insurance companies will help increase the transparency and accountability of domestic insurers. This may include requirements for board diversification, compensation policies, and ethical standards.

Introducing and tightening anti-corruption measures in the insurance industry will help create a more transparent and ethical business environment, which is an important part of ESG transformation.

Developing educational programs for insurance company employees and raising their awareness of the importance of ESG principles can be a key factor in the successful transformation of the industry.

The introduction of ESG principles in domestic insurance requires a comprehensive approach from regulators, insurance companies, and other stakeholders. Developing a clear regulatory framework, supporting responsible investment, and raising awareness of the importance of sustainable development are key elements of successful ESG transformation of the domestic insurance business. Participation in international initiatives and partnerships with international organizations can help in the exchange of experience and best practices in ESG transformation.

2.3 Features of ESG Transformation of the Domestic Insurance Business

ESG transformation in the insurance business in Uzbekistan is an important and relevant process within the framework of the country's overall adaptation to global sustainable development trends. In recent years, Uzbekistan has been actively developing the economy, strengthening the role of the private sector, and modernizing the legislative framework. In this context, the introduction of ESG principles (environmental, social, and governance responsibility) in the country's insurance sector becomes an important step in creating a competitive and sustainable market. Examples of the implementation of ESG environmental principles in the insurance market of Uzbekistan are provided in Table 2.5.

Uzbekistan, as a country with a predominantly agricultural sector and certain natural risks (such as the drying up of the Aral Sea), faces the need to consider environmental risks in its economy. Insurance companies can develop products aimed at protecting against natural disasters such as floods, droughts, or sandstorms that may affect agriculture and infrastructure.

It is also important to develop "green" insurance, which includes programs aimed at protecting the environment. For example, ecotourism insurance, clean technology insurance, and support for initiatives to improve environmental sustainability in the industry.

To reduce their carbon footprint, insurance companies can start to implement internal standards aimed at reducing energy consumption, using renewable sources, optimizing office processes, and reducing carbon emissions.

An example could be participation in national and international projects to stimulate the use of green and sustainable technologies throughout the country's economy.

Insurers can introduce discounts or bonuses for customers who drive eco-friendly cars or participate in waste-recycling programs. Such initiatives can help raise environmental awareness among the population.

Table 2.5. Examples of ESG environmental principles implementation in the insurance market of Uzbekistan.

Direction	Description	Examples in the Insurance Business of Uzbekistan
Environmental Risks Consideration	Introduction of products aimed at protection against natural disasters and environmental risks.	Insurance against risks related to drought, floods, sandstorms; development of agriculture policies.
Green Insurance	Insurance of projects aimed at sustainable development and environmental protection.	Programs for environmentally friendly technologies, eco-tourism, renewable energy sources.
Reducing carbon footprint	Reducing the impact on the climate and ecosystem through reducing carbon dioxide emissions.	Optimization of internal processes to reduce energy consumption; transition to renewable energy sources in offices.
Encouraging environmentally responsible behavior	Providing bonuses and discounts for environmentally conscious customers.	Discounts on insurance for electric vehicles, support for waste recycling programs.

Uzbekistan has a significant rural population and people with disabilities who need access to insurance coverage. Insurance companies should work to develop affordable products for all categories of the population, including through microinsurance development, development of life, health and disability insurance for vulnerable groups of the population, such as the elderly, low-income, and large families, as and the provision of various discounts and benefits for such categories.

Insurance companies in Uzbekistan can actively develop corporate social responsibility programs aimed at improving the social infrastructure in the country, such as assistance in the recovery of those affected by natural disasters, training and advanced training for young people.

It is also important to develop programs to support and protect workers' rights, fight discrimination, and support labor equality, as well as create safe and comfortable working conditions.

Insurance companies can actively participate in educational and awareness-raising projects aimed at raising public awareness of the importance of financial planning, health protection, and prevention of risks related to accidents and diseases.

Developing and supporting programs to prevent lifestyle-related diseases may be especially relevant in the context of fighting infectious diseases and improving the general health of the nation.

Examples of the implementation of the ESG social principles in the insurance market of Uzbekistan are given in Table 2.6.

In Uzbekistan, the insurance market is developing with a growing number of private companies, and increasing transparency is becoming an important factor in attracting foreign investment and raising customer confidence. Insurers should actively implement open and honest corporate governance practices and publish detailed reports on their activities, as well as on the compliance of ESG principles.

The development of international corporate governance standards, such as GRI (Global Reporting Initiative), can help insurance companies meet the requirements of global trends, foreign partners, and investors.

An important element of corporate governance is the development of effective risk management systems, especially in the context of environmental and social challenges.

Table 2.6. Examples of ESG social principles implementation in the insurance market of Uzbekistan.

Direction	**Description**	**Examples in the Insurance Business of Uzbekistan**
Accessibility and Inclusion	Developing products for various population groups, including vulnerable groups.	Microinsurance programs, affordable policies for low-income individuals, retired and large families.
Corporate Social Responsibility	Support of social infrastructure, development of personnel welfare.	Training and professional development programs for employees, creation of safe working conditions.
Education programs	Educational activities aimed at increasing financial literacy and awareness.	Educational campaigns on financial planning, training on the need for insurance.
Health and prevention programs	Implementation of programs aimed at improving public health.	Health insurance programs for disease prevention, support of a healthy lifestyle.

Insurance companies in Uzbekistan must take measures to comply with the norms and standards governing the insurance sector, as well as support policies to protect consumer rights and prevent fraud.

In recent years, Uzbekistan has taken steps to strengthen legislation to create incentives for the implementation of ESG practices in the insurance business.

To improve their reputation and reliability, domestic insurance companies can cooperate with international organizations and initiatives in the field of sustainable development, such as PRI (Principles for Responsible Investment), which will help create a management system that takes into account environmental and social risks.

Examples of the implementation of ESG management principles in the insurance market of Uzbekistan are given in Table 2.7.

ESG transformation in Uzbekistan faces a number of challenges, including insufficient awareness of sustainable development principles, the absence of a clear regulatory framework, issues with the introduction of green technologies, and social justice. The issues and challenges of ESG transformation of the insurance market of Uzbekistan are presented in Table 2.8.

Despite the global trend, in Uzbekistan, there is still insufficient awareness among both companies and consumers regarding ESG principles. This requires active educational and information campaigns.

A comprehensive regulatory framework governing ESG principles in the insurance sector has not yet been formed, which complicates the implementation of relevant practices.

Lack of specialized products: Insurance products focused on environmental and social responsibility are being developed, and the market may lack suitable proposals for certain groups of people and businesses. However, with the adoption of comprehensive measures to improve the environmental, social, and governance infrastructure, the country can successfully develop sustainable development principles, which will contribute not only to environmental and social stability but also to improving competitiveness in international markets.

Table 2.7. Examples of the implementation of ESG management principles in the insurance market of Uzbekistan.

Direction	Description	Examples in the Insurance Business of Uzbekistan
Transparency and accountability	Implementation of reporting and transparency practices in the activities of companies, compliance with international standards	Publication of annual reports, including information on ESG principles compliance, and audit of corporate reports
Risk management	Developing effective risk management systems for environmental and social issues	Assessment and analysis of risks related to natural disasters, social issues, and implementation of systems for their monitoring
Compliance with the law	Compliance with the rules and standards governing the insurance market, including ESG principles	Development of internal policies for legislation compliance, cooperation with international regulators
Corporate Ethics and Anti-Corruption	Developing ethics codes, raising employee conduct standards	Implementation of anti-corruption policies, support for ethical standards in management, and interaction with clients

Table 2.8. Issues and challenges of ESG transformation of the insurance market of Uzbekistan.

Issue	Description	Solutions and Approaches
Low awareness of ESG principles	Many organizations do not understand or are not sufficiently aware of the importance of ESG for their business	Educational and information campaigns, advanced training of insurance company employees
Lack of developed regulatory framework	The legislative framework in the ESG principles area is not yet developed, which makes it difficult to implement these practices	Development and implementation of new standards, creation of public and private partnerships to stimulate ESG practices
Shortage of specialized products	There may not be enough supply of environmentally and socially responsible insurance on the market	Development of new products and services complying with ESG principles (e.g. green insurance)

Table 2.9. Prospects and trends of ESG transformation in the insurance market of Uzbekistan.

Trend	Description	Examples
Foreign investors' growing interest	ESG principles' implementation increases attractiveness for foreign investors and partners	Attracting investments into sustainable projects such as green insurance, infrastructure projects
Digitalization and innovation	Development of new technologies such as artificial intelligence and blockchain contributes to the ESG practice improvement	Introduction of automated systems for risk monitoring, ESG reporting digitalization
State support and incentives	Increased government attention is given to sustainable business development, including the insurance sector	Tax incentives and subsidy programs for companies that actively implement environmentally sustainable and socially responsible practices

The implementation of ESG principles can help attract foreign investors to Uzbekistan's insurance sector, as international investors increasingly look for projects that take into account environmental and social responsibility.

In recent years, sustainability principles, including environmental, social, and governance (ESG) aspects, have become an integral part of the various industries' transformation, including insurance. The introduction of ESG principles in the insurance business is an important step toward sustainable and socially responsible economic development.

Particular attention should be paid to the role of digital technologies, such as blockchain, in improving transparency, process efficiency, and customer experience in this area. In the future, significant changes can be expected through legislative and tax support for companies actively implementing ESG practices. Given the current challenges and opportunities, the introduction of ESG principles in the insurance sector of Uzbekistan is an important part of the country's economic transformation aimed at sustainable development. The prospects and trends of ESG transformation in the insurance market of Uzbekistan are presented in Table 2.9.

The development of digital technologies in insurance (for example, the use of blockchain to improve transparency) can be an important tool for introducing ESG principles into the industry. This will increase the efficiency of insurance processes, reduce costs, and improve the customer experience.

In the future, it can be expected that government support and incentives for the implementation of sustainable development principles in business (including the insurance sector) will lead to the introduction of new legislative and tax incentives for companies actively implementing ESG practices.

Thus, in Uzbekistan, the introduction of ESG principles into the insurance business is an important part of the economic transformation toward sustainable development. Given the existing challenges and opportunities, this process will take time, but it will open new horizons for sustainable and socially responsible business.

Implementing sustainable development principles in the insurance business of Uzbekistan is a long-term task requiring time and effort from both businesses and the government. Digital technologies such as blockchain can be an important tool for increasing the transparency and efficiency of insurance processes, which in turn will help improve customer experience and reduce costs. In addition, government support, including legislative and tax incentives, will play a key role in stimulating the implementation of ESG principles in business.

In the future, this process will lead to the creation of a more responsible, transparent, and sustainable business, which will open new horizons for the economic development of Uzbekistan and will affect the improvement of the social and environmental situation in the country. The insurance sector, as one of the most important components of the economy, can play a leading role in this transformation, stimulating the transition to sustainable development and socially responsible business.

2.4 Conclusions

1. The economic essence of the ESG transformation of insurance business lies in a deep restructuring of the strategic and operational models of insurance companies, taking into account environmental, social, and governance (ESG) factors. This transformation rethinks traditional criteria for the insurance business effectiveness, complementing financial indicators with metrics of sustainable development and social responsibility. The basis contains the systemic integration of the principles of environmental responsibility (reducing carbon footprint, investing in green assets, considering climate risks), social inclusion (insurance coverage for vulnerable groups, ensuring equality and working conditions), as well as corporate governance (transparency, anti-corruption mechanisms, compliance with international reporting standards).

   The targets of the insurance sector's ESG transformation cover the formation of sustainable investment portfolios, digitalization of processes, introduction of risk-oriented assessment models, and strengthening of the internal corporate culture of sustainable development. The ESG approach is becoming a key tool for enhancing the competitiveness, investment attractiveness, and social legitimacy of insurance organizations, especially in the context of global climate instability and growing regulatory requirements.

   ESG transformation is not a fashionable trend, but an economically sound, long-term strategy for enhancing sustainability, transparency, and trust in insurance institutions, contributing to the modernization of the national insurance sector in accordance with the global challenges of the 21st century.
2. The regional specifics of ESG transformation regulations in the insurance sector reflect the diversity of legal regimes, economic priorities, and institutional capabilities.

The European Union demonstrates the most mature and systematic approach based on the regulatory integration of ESG principles into financial regulation and disclosure practices. In North America, a fragmented model dominates, combining initiatives of individual states and pressure from institutional investors and civil society. The Asia-Pacific region is characterized by high regulatory activity of leading economies with simultaneous regulatory heterogeneity. In Latin America and Africa, ESG regulations are in their early stages, with the main focus being on the social aspects of sustainability. Central Asia, although in the phase of institutional development of the ESG framework, shows signs of gradual adaptation under the influence of international organizations and global standards. ESG introduction in insurance requires not only regulatory unification and adaptation of international standards but also stimulation of industry transformation through financial, managerial, and educational instruments.

3. ESG transformation of the insurance business of Uzbekistan is an integral component of the process of sustainable modernization of the national economy. The introduction of environmental, social, and governance principles in the insurance sector helps to increase the adaptability of the industry to natural and climate risks, expand social inclusiveness, and institutionally strengthen corporate governance. The development of "green" insurance and support for vulnerable populations, ensuring transparency and compliance with ethical standards, form the basis for the sustainable competitiveness of insurance companies. Digitalization and technological innovations, including the introduction of blockchain, act as catalysts for the effectiveness of ESG practices. Despite institutional and regulatory constraints, the development of a system approach to ESG, supported by government incentives and international cooperation, opens up prospects for integrating the Uzbek insurance market into global sustainable financial flows.

Chapter 3

Methodology of ESG Transformation of Insurance Business

3.1 ESG Principles Evolution in the Insurance Business

The methodology of ESG transformation for the insurance business is a multi-level and comprehensive process aimed at integrating ESG principles into the strategic planning and operational processes of insurance companies. Successful ESG transformation requires the use of a structured methodology that covers the evolution of ESG principles in the insurance business, the ESG transformation strategy of the insurer, and ESG risks assessment in the Uzbek insurance market.

Understanding the evolution of ESG principles is impossible without taking into account the historical background that shaped the concept of sustainable development and is associated with the development of environmental and social responsibility of business. One of the key events that influenced the global perception of environmental and social risks was the UN Conference on the Environment, held in Stockholm in 1972.

This was the first large-scale international meeting to discuss global environmental issues such as environmental pollution and natural resource depletion. The Stockholm Conference became the starting point for further development of the sustainable development concept and the formation of international environmental policy.

The conference played a key role in understanding the need to adopt international standards and mechanisms aimed at environmental protection, which later became the basis for the formation of eco-oriented strategies in various industries, including insurance. The environmental principles developed during this conference also became the basis for incorporating sustainability into corporate activities, including environmental risk assessment and the development of appropriate insurance products.

The evolution of ESG principles in the insurance business has been taking place over the past several decades, with corresponding global changes in the economy, public consciousness, and the legislative environment. The stages of the ESG principles' evolution in the insurance business are presented in Table 3.1.

In the early stages of implementing ESG principles in the insurance business, i.e. in the 1990s and early 2000s, the emphasis was placed primarily on the economic aspects of companies' activities. At that time, sustainable development, covering environmental and social issues, remained a secondary element. Most insurance companies focused on traditional financial indicators such as profit, assets, and capital, without considering long-term environmental or social risks.

However, with the development of international regulatory mechanisms and increased attention to the issues of global warming, climate change, and economic sustainability,

Table 3.1. ESG principles evolution stages in the insurance business.

Stage	Year	Main Events and Initiatives	Impact on Insurance Business
Early stage	1990s	Stockholm Environment Conference (1972)	The start of awareness of the need to take into account environmental risks in insurance
First steps	2000s	Introduction of international agreements such as the Kyoto Protocol (1997) and sustainable investment standards development	Developing the first insurance products for protection against climate risks
ESG integration	2010s	Paris Agreement (2015), growing interest in green Investments	Introduction of environmental and social principles into the strategies of insurance companies
Modern stage	2020s and further	Strengthening ESG reporting requirements, developing sustainable insurance	Full ESG integration into corporate strategies, development of innovative products

there was a need to take into account risks related to environmental factors. At this time, it became obvious that climate change, such as floods, hurricanes, and other natural disasters, can significantly affect the financial condition of insurance companies, which required changes in risk assessment models.

Since the early 2000s, global changes in the legislative and economic spheres have contributed to a more active implementation of ESG principles in the activities of companies. Growing awareness that sustainable development is linked to long-term business profitability has encouraged insurance companies to integrate environmental and social risks into their strategies and operations. One of the significant steps at this stage was the inclusion of environmental sustainability principles in companies' strategies.

Particular attention was paid to ecology, primarily to assessing risks related to climate change. For example, insurance against natural disasters became one of the key areas in which climate risk data was actively used. During this period, special insurance products aimed at reducing the consequences of disasters caused by climate change, such as hurricanes, floods, and earthquakes, began to be actively developed.

In addition, there were initial efforts to implement corporate reporting standards aimed at increasing transparency and improving stakeholder engagement. Insurance companies began publishing reports that took into account not only financial results but also indicators related to the environmental and social aspects of their activities.

Between 2010 and 2020, ESG principles became an integral part of the strategy and corporate culture of the leading global insurance companies. This stage is characterized by the growing importance of ESG factors for long-term business development. The establishment of international standards, such as the Paris Climate Agreement (2015) and the adoption of the Principles of Responsible Investment (PRI), encouraged companies to actively include ESG-oriented goals in their strategic plans.

The ecological component in this context continues to be the most evident. Insurance companies have begun to actively work with risks related to climate change and develop

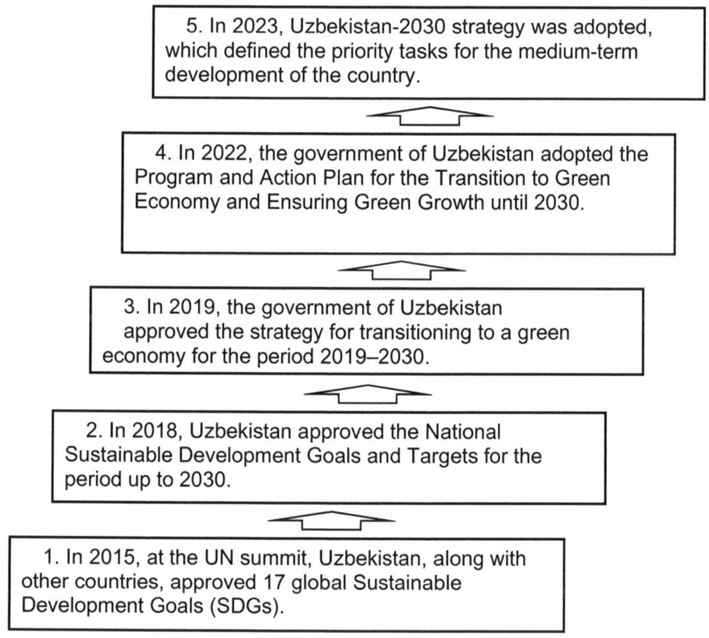

Fig. 3.1. Evolution of Uzbekistan on the path of ESG transformation and sustainable development.
Source: Developed by the author based on the Decrees and Resolutions of the President and the Government of the Republic of Uzbekistan.

appropriate products to protect clients from environmental disasters. In addition, interest in investing in environmentally sustainable projects has increased, including renewable energy projects, sustainable construction, and carbon emissions reduction. During this period, attention to social aspects, such as human rights protection, support for diversity, and inclusion in corporate governance, has also increased significantly.

Since the early 2020s, ESG principles have become a central part of the strategy of most insurance companies around the world. This process is supported by both internal and external factors. Insurance companies increasingly began to comprehend that corporate responsibility in the areas of ecology, social issues, and governance significantly affects their long-term competitiveness and ability to attract investors.

At this stage, it is fundamentally important to note several key trends:

- Environmental sustainability: Insurance companies continued to develop products aimed at reducing the risks related to natural disasters, including innovative products such as insurance against environmental risks related to climate change. There is also a growing trend toward investing in "green" projects, including renewable energy and sustainable agriculture.
- Social responsibility: Emphasis on the social factor becomes more pronounced. Along this direction, insurance companies began to develop products aimed at improving the quality of life, including affordable health insurance, as well as support for social and educational initiatives. It is important to note that social sustainability also becomes part of the internal corporate culture, where companies strive to support diversity, inclusion, and equality among employees.
- Corporate governance: Insurance companies began to pay more attention to transparency and ethical practices in corporate governance. This includes fighting corruption,

improving internal reporting, and strengthening interactions with regulators and stakeholders.

One of the most important elements of this process is the increase in the level of ESG principles reporting. Leading insurance companies have begun to implement disclosure systems that include not only financial results but also indicators related to their impact on the environment, society, and corporate governance. Such reports are becoming an important tool both for increasing transparency and for attracting investors interested in sustainable and ethical business practices.

The stages of the ESG principles' evolution in the insurance business are presented in Table 3.1. The prospects for the development of ESG principles in the insurance business include further integration of environmental, social, and management sustainability into strategic and operational processes of companies. The following are expected in the future:

- The development of new innovative products will continue, aimed at minimizing the risks related to climate change and environmental degradation.
- The digitalization of processes will play an important role and will allow for better integration of ESG factors into risk assessments and decision-making processes.
- ESG principles disclosure requirements will continue to grow, contributing to improved transparency and increased trust among customers and investors.
- There will be greater cooperation between insurance companies and governments to address global challenges such as climate change and social inequality.

Thus, the evolution of ESG principles in the insurance business demonstrates the importance of sustainable development for the long-term viability of companies. The introduction of environmental, social, and management values into corporate strategies is becoming not only a trend but a necessity to ensure competitiveness in the context of global challenges of our time.

In recent years, Uzbekistan has significantly increased its efforts to transit to a "green" economy and sustainable development, which has become an important part of the state's strategy. This process has become especially relevant due to global challenges related to climate change, natural resource depletion, and the need to improve the quality of life of the people. Sustainable development covers not only environmental aspects but also social and management factors, which requires a comprehensive approach to transforming all sectors of the economy.

In the early stages, Uzbekistan focused on economic growth and industrial modernization, which contributed to basic infrastructure improvements, but sustainability and environmental issues were not on the agenda. The environmental situation, including issues related to the drying up of the Aral Sea and water resources pollution, attracted only limited attention. Following this period, the country began to pay more attention to environmental issues. An important step in this direction was Uzbekistan's participation in international initiatives to combat climate change, such as signing various agreements on environmental protection and sustainable development. During this period, programs to improve the environment, save energy, and create "green" jobs began to be actively implemented.

In 2015, Uzbekistan joined the Paris Agreement on Climate Change, which became an important step toward a green economy. Due to global changes and the need to adapt to environmental challenges, the country began to actively develop and implement national sustainable development programs, including the development of renewable energy sources, measures to increase energy efficiency, and improvements in environmental infrastructure. One of the significant steps was the adoption of the Sustainable

Development Concept of the Republic of Uzbekistan until 2030, focusing on environmental safety, natural resource protection, the development of green technologies, and ensuring social justice.

In recent years, Uzbekistan has continued to deepen its efforts to integrate ESG principles into the economy. One of the most important elements of the sustainable development strategy has become the formation of conditions for a large-scale transition to a "green" economy, which involves not only the introduction of environmentally friendly technologies but also the active inclusion of social and management aspects into corporate practice and public policy. Particular attention is paid to improving the quality of life for citizens through sustainable social projects, increasing transparency in the management of natural resources, and effective cooperation with international organizations.

The integration of ESG principles into the economy is also seen in the financial sector, including the insurance business. Insurance companies in Uzbekistan are gradually beginning to take into account ESG risks by developing new insurance products and risk assessment methodologies. For example, companies have begun to introduce environmental insurance, including insurance against natural disasters, and develop products aimed at promoting social sustainability (for example, health and life insurance for the population).

The insurance market transformation within the ESG principles framework in Uzbekistan also includes the need to increase reporting transparency and adapt to international standards. Insurers focusing on sustainable development principles can improve their reputation and attract international investment, which is especially important for emerging markets.

The evolution of ESG principles in the insurance business of Uzbekistan reflects global trends adapted to national realities. Over the past few years, there has been an increase in awareness among insurance market participants about the importance of sustainable development and the integration of ESG approaches into strategy and operational processes.

Further, this evolution requires consolidation of efforts by the state, businesses, and society. The introduction of ESG principles will strengthen the reputation of insurance companies and will also become an important tool for achieving sustainable socio-economic development of the country.

The historical background of the formation of sustainable development concepts and the ESG transformation of the insurance business can be considered the result of a long-term evolutionary process based on the interaction of economic, social, and environmental factors. Ultimately, the implementation of ESG principles will allow for building a safer and more sustainable future for both businesses and society as a whole. This is not merely compliance with requirements but an opportunity for insurance companies to take a leading position in the new economy based on the principles of sustainable development and social responsibility. Such companies are able to protect their interests and make significant contributions to solving global issues, making them more attractive to clients and investors in the long term.

3.2 ESG Transformation Strategy for Insurers in a Transition Economy

In transition economies, such as Uzbekistan, the implementation of ESG principles is a key factor contributing to the sustainable development of the insurance sector and its adaptation to modern global challenges. ESG principles are becoming an important tool that helps companies not only meet the growing demands of stakeholders but also increase their market competitiveness, strengthen their reputation, and attract international investment. The implementation of these principles in the insurance business helps reduce risks related to ESG aspects and also opens up new opportunities for innovative insurance products and services.

However, this implementation in emerging countries, such as Uzbekistan, is accompanied by a number of specific challenges caused by several factors. Firstly, a lack of financial and institutional resources complicates the implementation of comprehensive ESG programs in insurance companies. Secondly, in many markets, including Uzbekistan, low awareness of sustainable development principles and their importance for businesses limits the active implementation of ESG principles in practice. Thirdly, at the level of legislation and the regulatory framework, there is a limitation or insufficiency of regulations governing the implementation of ESG standards in corporate governance, reducing the motivation of companies to actively use these principles.

In this regard, the task of selecting the optimal ESG transformation strategy for insurers in the context of the transition economy is particularly relevant. The strategy should not only be adapted to the market specifics but also take into account international trends, as well as the needs and expectations of stakeholders, such as government agencies, investors, clients, and company personnel. At the same time, it is necessary to consider the fact that successful ESG transformation requires a comprehensive approach, which includes environmentally oriented product development, social initiative implementations, corporate governance improvements, and increased transparency and reporting by companies.

In addition, a key aspect is the development of financial instruments supporting ESG initiatives, which requires the formation of favorable conditions to attract external investment, stimulating private and public partnerships, and using international experience in the field of sustainable development. Thus, the development and implementation of ESG transformation strategies require a balanced approach, taking into account the unique conditions of the transition economy and the need to create a strong institutional and regulatory framework to support the sustainable development of the insurance sector.

The ESG transformation strategy of the insurer is a systematic, long-term, and multilevel approach to implementing sustainable development principles in the insurance company's activities. It is aimed at integrating three key aspects: environmental, social, and governance. This strategy forms the basis for increasing the sustainability of the business, its social responsibility, and its competitiveness in the modern market.

The environmental component of the insurer's ESG transformation strategy involves developing and implementing solutions that minimize negative impacts on the environment and promote sustainable development. This may include the following:

- development of insurance products aimed at managing climate risks, protecting environmental assets, and supporting green technologies;
- participation in the financing of projects related to renewable energy, sustainable construction, and carbon footprint reduction;
- optimization of internal processes, for example, paper use reduction through digitalization and the introduction of energy-efficient technologies.

The social component of the strategy is aimed at supporting inclusiveness, increasing the insurance services availability, and improving interaction with various population groups. The main objectives include the following:

- insurance coverage expansion through micro insurance, accessible to vulnerable groups;
- educational programs to improve financial literacy among the population;
- formation of an inclusive corporate culture that supports equality, gender diversity, and employee well-being.

The goal of the ESG transformation strategy is to create a sustainable development system for insurance company that:

- meets regulatory requirements and public expectations;
- increases the long-term economic value of the company;
- promotes development of social and environmental responsibility of the business.

The objectives of the strategy include the following:

- formation of a new corporate culture based on ESG principles;
- increasing the efficiency of business processes through digitalization and resource optimization;
- strengthening the trust of clients, partners, and investors through transparency and regular reporting.

A block diagram of the algorithm for developing an ESG transformation strategy for insurers is presented in Fig. 3.2.

Assessing and analyzing insurers' existing ESG practices is key to understanding how insurers address sustainability challenges and what practices can be transferred to other organizations. Let's look at the main aspects of this assessment.

Many insurers have started to integrate ESG principles into their business processes. This includes assessments related to climate change and adapting insurance products to support sustainable practices. Insurers are offering new insurance products such as renewable energy policies, environmental risk insurance, and programs to support customers implementing sustainable technologies. For example, Allianz and AXA have developed specialized products to cover risks related to solar and wind installations. This not only reduces risks for customers but also supports the transition to sustainable energy sources.

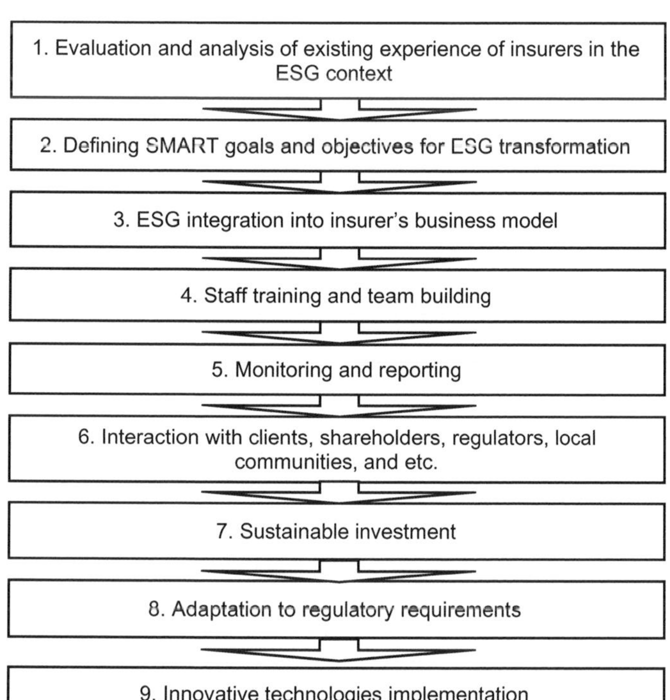

Fig. 3.2. Block diagram of the algorithm for ESG transformation strategy development for insurers.

The issues at this stage of developing an insurer's ESG transformation strategy include the lack of universal standards for assessing ESG practices in insurance, which makes it difficult to compare and analyze data among different insurance companies. In addition, assessing the results of an insurer's ESG transformation can be difficult due to the lack of clear metrics and methodologies.

Assessment of the existing experience of insurers in the context of ESG transformation shows that many companies are already taking steps to integrate sustainable practices into their activities. The common standards development, investment in technology, and employee training will help improve ESG transformation efficiency and strengthen the position of insurers in the market.

Defining SMART goals and objectives for an insurer's ESG transformation is an important step for the successful implementation of sustainable practices. This allows insurers to build a clear and structured basis for implementing sustainable practices. These goals help not only improve internal processes but also increase the company's competitiveness in the market, meeting the requirements of customers and investors.

The integration of ESG principles into an insurer's business model is crucial for ensuring sustainable growth and competitiveness in today's marketplace. This process requires a comprehensive and consistent approach. It increases the sustainability and competitiveness of the business and contributes to creating a positive impact on society and the environment. Implementing ESG strategies will help insurers adapt to changes in the marketplace and customer expectations, ensuring long-term success and sustainable development.

Staff training and the formation of a dedicated team for ESG transformation are key aspects for successful integration of sustainable practices into an insurer's operations. These measures help to increase awareness, engagement, and the ability of personnel to adapt to new conditions.

The measures are critical for successful integration of sustainable practices into a business model as well. They help to foster a corporate culture focused on sustainable development and contribute to improving relationships with clients and stakeholders. A strong team prepared to implement ESG initiatives will be able to effectively cope with challenges and seize new opportunities, ensuring the long-term success of the insurer.

Effective monitoring and reporting on ESG transformation are critical to assessing the success of integrating sustainable practices into an insurer's business model. These processes not only track progress against targets but also demonstrate transparency and reporting to stakeholders.

Some of the clear, measurable metrics to assess the success of the insurer's ESG transformation could include:

- carbon footprint reduction (e.g. in tons of CO_2),
- the share of ESG products in the portfolio,
- the level of personnel engagement in ESG initiatives (e.g. participation in trainings),
- the number of social projects supported by the company.

Effective monitoring systems, clear KPIs, and transparent reporting help not only track progress but also demonstrate responsibility to stakeholders. This approach helps strengthen the insurer's reputation and creates additional value for clients and investors.

Effective stakeholder engagement is an important aspect of an insurer's ESG transformation. This engagement helps build trust, ensures support for initiatives, and adapts strategies to the expectations and demands of various groups. Engagement with customers, shareholders, regulators, and local communities is an important aspect of an insurer's ESG transformation. Effective communication and collaboration with these groups helps build trust, improve reputation, and create additional value for all stakeholders. This approach not only increases business sustainability but also helps create a positive impact on society and the environment.

Sustainable investing is becoming an important element of an insurer's ESG transformation, ensuring not only financial stability but also compliance with modern sustainable development requirements. This approach helps manage risks and create long-term value, taking into account ESG factors.

Sustainable investing is not just a choice but a strategic necessity for insurers seeking to adapt to changing market conditions and social expectations. Effective integration of ESG principles into an investment strategy minimizes risks, as well as creates competitive advantages, contributing to financial stability and improving the company's reputation. This approach allows insurers to not only achieve short-term results but also build a sustainable future focused on long-term value for all stakeholders.

Adaptation to regulatory requirements as part of the insurer's ESG transformation is a key element in the successful integration of sustainable practices into the business model. Effective implementation of this task reduces legal and financial risks; it also strengthens the company's reputation as a responsible and reliable market participant.

A proactive approach to regulatory compliance allows insurers to:

- adapt to change: react quickly to new requirements and standards, avoiding potential fines and ensuring the smooth functioning of the business;
- increase trust: commitment to high ESG compliance standards helps to gain the trust of customers, investors, and shareholders, which in turn helps to strengthen the customer base and increase investment attractiveness;
- promote innovation and competitiveness: compliance with regulatory requirements often requires the implementation of new solutions and business process optimization, which not only ensures compliance but can also become a competitive advantage;
- meet stakeholder expectations: transparency and openness about ESG compliance create a favorable environment for deeper engagement with customers, shareholders, and local communities, which helps to build long-term partnerships.

Thus, ESG transformation improves the insurer's internal processes and also opens up new opportunities for sustainable growth and development in a rapidly changing world, where sustainable development becomes a priority for the insurance business.

The introduction of innovative technologies is a key component of the insurer's ESG transformation, contributing to increased business sustainability, operational efficiency, and compliance with modern sustainable development requirements. The integration of advanced technologies not only helps achieve ESG goals but also creates significant competitive advantages in the market. These technologies play a decisive role in ensuring the sustainability and competitiveness of insurers. They allow for internal process optimization, customer experience improvement, and effective risk management. Increasing the operational transparency also helps to strengthen the trust of customers and regulators.

Successful integration of innovative technologies helps insurers adapt to rapidly changing conditions of sustainable development and meet the expectations of stakeholders. This not only improves financial results but also contributes to the formation of a company's positive image as a socially responsible and reliable market participant, creating long-term value for all parties involved. The algorithm for developing an ESG transformation strategy, which we proposed earlier, will allow the insurer to both implement ESG principles and build a sustainable business model, meeting the needs of customers and society, which in turn will enhance its reputation and competitiveness in the market.

The ESG transformation strategy of an insurer is an important tool for adapting the insurance business to the challenges of the modern global economy. It is aimed at forming the long-term sustainability of the company and its contribution to achieving sustainable development goals. The application of such a strategy requires a comprehensive approach, including taking into account the interests of all stakeholders, introducing innovations, and constantly monitoring the results achieved.

3.3 ESG Risk Assessment in the Insurance Market of Uzbekistan

The ESG principles implementation in the insurance sector of Uzbekistan is related to a number of ESG risks that must be taken into account and minimized for successful sustainable development implementation.

The environmental component of the ESG transformation is especially important in the context of changes in natural and climate conditions, as well as in the framework of increasing attention of the world community to environmental protection and sustainability issues. Uzbekistan, being the most populous country in Central Asia, is a landlocked country. Geographically, the republic is located between the Amu Darya and Syr Darya rivers. With a total area of 448.9 thousand square kilometers, of which 425.4 thousand square kilometers are land and 22 thousand square kilometers are water, the country's territory stretches 1,425 km from west to east and 930 km from north to south. The country has long borders with neighboring states: Kazakhstan (2,203 km), Turkmenistan (1,621 km), Tajikistan (1,161 km), Kyrgyzstan (1,099 km), and Afghanistan (137 km) (Fig. 3.3.).

Fig. 3.3. Location of the Republic of Uzbekistan.[1]

[1] https://saletur.ru/galery/tfoto_map/big/3671.jpg.

Uzbekistan has a sharply continental climate: The average temperature can drop to −6°C in January and reach +32°C in July. Precipitation is relatively low, ranging from 120 to 200 mm in lowland areas to 1000 mm in mountainous regions. This climatic feature makes the country's agriculture highly dependent on irrigation. The main rivers feeding the territory of Uzbekistan are the Amu Darya and Syr Darya, the total lengths of which are 1437 and 2137 km, respectively. There are also large artificial reservoirs in the country, such as the Chardara and Charvak reservoirs.

Uzbekistan has significant natural and mineral potential, which includes rich deposits of precious, non-ferrous, and rare metals and hydrocarbon raw materials (oil and gas), as well as brown coal and uranium ores. The Republic occupies high positions in the world rankings for reserves and production of natural resources such as gold (16th place by reserves and 9th place by production), natural gas (16th place by production), copper (11th place by reserves), and uranium (10th place by production).

Uzbekistan, like other Central Asian countries, is exposed to risks related to natural disasters. The country has a history of various natural disasters, including earthquakes, landslides, avalanches, floods, and droughts. These disasters are inevitable consequences of Uzbekistan's unique geographical location and the region's climate.

In this regard, it is important to consider ESG risks, which have a significant impact on the country's insurance market. Vulnerability to natural disasters requires insurance companies to develop comprehensive strategies to assess and minimize ESG risks.

The tense environmental situation in the region and other countries of the world, caused by both natural and anthropogenic factors, requires the development of new approaches to solving this issue. One such approach is the use of insurance mechanisms.

Natural disasters such as earthquakes, landslides, mudflows, floods, and droughts pose significant threats in Uzbekistan. Among them, earthquakes are the most destructive in their effects.

For example, powerful earthquakes occurred in the 20th century in cities such as Andijan (1902), Tashkent (1946 and 1966), and Gazli (1976 and 1984), which caused significant economic losses and numerous casualties. These events highlight the need to develop and implement effective insurance mechanisms to minimize damage from natural disasters and protect the population and the economy from such threats. The history of crises and natural disasters is presented in Table 3.2.

The Tashkent earthquake in 1966 caused total damage estimated at US$300 million. Adjusted for inflation and recalculated to 2008 prices, the losses from that earthquake would have been around US$2 billion. In the event of a similar event today, the losses would likely be significantly higher, given the significant increase in the value of properties at risk in the capital.

In addition, according to the World Bank, UNISDR, and CAREC estimates, average annual economic losses from natural disasters in Uzbekistan amount to at least US$92 million. In absolute terms, this amount is the highest among Central Asian countries, which highlights the urgency of developing effective risk management and insurance measures to minimize economic damage from natural disasters.

The economic losses due to disasters, given their occurrence probability, have significant implications for various industries, including the insurance sector. Experts estimate that damage from a disaster with a five-year frequency (i.e. with an annual probability exceeding 20%) could be approximately US$177 million. In turn, for a disaster with a one-in-200-year frequency (with an annual probability exceeding 0.5%), expected losses could exceed US$2 billion, which is approximately 9.5% of the country's gross domestic product (GDP).

Table 3.2. History of crises and disasters.

No.	Date of Incidents	Description of Consequences
1.	May 4, 1991	As a result of heavy rains and seismic impacts, a landslide occurred in the territory of the Jigaristan village in Angren city in the Tashkent region. Losses: 60 people died, more than 400 people were evacuated, and houses, buildings, and other structures were damaged.
2.	June 8, 1998	Heavy snowmelt caused a lake located in Kyrgyzstan to overflow. As a result, the volume of water in the Shakhimardan-Sai River, which flows in the Fergana district of the Fergana region, increased. More than 100 people died as a result of the mudflow.
3.	July 20, 2011	As a result of the earthquake in Kyrgyzstan (the epicenter is Sovetsky village), more than 15 people died and about 50 were injured.
4.	February 18, 2012	Due to a sharp air temperature increase and precipitation that occurred in the Gallaoral district of the Jizzakh region, mudflows passed along the floodplain of the Karasoy River, causing significant damage to houses and farms. More than 1,300 people were evacuated.
5.	May 26, 2013	An earthquake occurred, the epicenter of which was in Uzbekistan (magnitude 6.2 points). As a result, more than 1,500 economic and social facilities were damaged. The material damage amounted to more than 55 billion Soums.
6.	April 27, 2020	A cyclone with strong winds entered from the territory of Turkmenistan with gusts of 9–40 m/s. In Bukhara, 41,085 households were affected by the natural disaster. The total amount of material damage amounted to 140 billion Soums.
7.	May 1, 2020	As a result of the dam break in the Sardoba reservoir in the Syrdarya region of the country, more than 70,000 residents in flooded settlements in three districts of the region suffered. 4,351 residential buildings, 24 bridges, and 276 km of roads were flooded or damaged. In Kazakhstan, five villages were flooded, more than 31 thousand residents were evacuated, and 845 residential buildings were flooded. Losses and expenses amounted to more than 1.5 trillion Soums.

Source: Developed by the author based on the World Bank report "Property Insurance against Disasters in the Republic of Uzbekistan", January 2020 https://documents1.worldbank.org/curated/en/617231591599422910/pdf/Disaster-Property-Insurance-in-Uzbekistan-Overview-and-Recommendations.pdf.

Insurance companies must recognize that their activities and strategies impact not only the economy but also the country's ecosystem and climate resilience, posing challenges both to the traditional business sphere and to environmental matters.

One of the most significant environmental risks for the insurance market is the climate change impact, which leads to an increase in the frequency and intensity of extreme weather events such as floods, droughts, earthquakes, strong winds, and other natural disasters. These changes cause additional risks for insurance companies, which may face an increase in the number of insurance claims, as well as an increase in the size of insurance claims. In Uzbekistan, as in other countries, climate change can lead to serious consequences for agriculture, infrastructure, and residential areas, which will directly affect insurance companies. In response to these risks, insurers must develop adaptive strategies, including increasing policy prices, creating new insurance types for risks related to climate change, and introducing stricter conditions for clients who do not comply with environmental standards.

A major environmental risk for the insurance sector is environmental pollution caused by both individuals and corporate clients. Insurance companies may be required to cover damages related to pollutant emissions, water pollution, and land pollution, which will result in significant financial costs. In the case of major environmental disasters, such as chemical pollution or oil spills, insurance companies must be prepared to compensate for losses for both individuals and large enterprises. As ESG standards evolve, insurers will have to implement stricter criteria for assessing environmental risks in their products, including mandatory verification of environmental standards and green investments. In addition, companies must take into account environmental obligations, which may require additional costs to ensure the environmental responsibility of their clients.

In the context of global trends and increasing pressure from international organizations and national governments, the insurance sector must adapt to new environmental standards and regulations aimed at reducing carbon emissions, increasing energy efficiency, and protecting ecosystems. Insurance companies that are not prepared to quickly implement these standards risk facing fines, restrictions, or loss of competitiveness. The introduction of environmental standards into the economy is relatively new in Uzbekistan, and there is a risk that the regulatory framework will not comply with international environmental requirements, which could become an obstacle to sustainable practices development in the insurance sector. To minimize this risk, companies need to actively monitor changes in legislation and adapt their internal processes and standards to environmental sustainability requirements.

Insurance companies face difficulties in the proper assessment of the environmental impact of their clients, particularly in natural resource extraction, manufacturing, and agriculture. Insurers must introduce methods to assess the potential impact of environmental risks and take them into account when writing policies. For example, companies must develop special risk assessment models for agriculture in drought- or flood-prone areas and for industrial facilities whose activities may be related to high pollution levels. Failure to adequately assess environmental risks can lead to miscalculations and increased risk of losses.

When implementing ESG principles in the insurance sector, it is important to consider not only short-term environmental risks but also long-term sustainability consequences. Insurance companies that do not actively engage in supporting environmental initiatives and do not consider the long-term environmental impacts of their activities may face reputational risks. For example, failure to make green investments or develop products that meet sustainability standards may lead to a decrease in trust from customers and investors, which will negatively affect the company's position in the market. It is important for insurers to develop long-term strategies aimed at supporting environmental initiatives, such as insuring green projects, switching to renewable energy sources, and promoting biodiversity preservation.

Environmental risks in the ESG transformation of the insurance market of Uzbekistan require a comprehensive approach to their assessment and minimization and management. To effectively implement sustainable development in the insurance sector, it is necessary to take into account climate and natural changes, introduce innovative technologies for environmental risk management, and actively work to improve environmental responsibility standards both at the company level and at the level of legislation and society as a whole.

One of the key factors influencing the ESG transformation of the insurance business in Uzbekistan is the insufficient level of real income among the population, limiting accessibility of insurance services for a significant portion of the population. Another important factor is the low level of insurance culture and trust from insureds in financial and insurance institutions, which complicates traditional insurance development. These circumstances have a negative impact on the insurance sector's development and delay the effective implementation of strategies aimed at sustainable development and socially responsible behavior.

Social risks arising in the process of implementing ESG principles (environmental, social, and governance responsibility) in the insurance market of Uzbekistan are an important and multifaceted aspect requiring deep analysis. Sustainable development in this context is impossible without taking into account the impact on social structures, interactions with society, issues related to social justice and equality, and the involvement of various population segments. In conditions of active ESG transformation, social risks can have a significant impact on the success and effectiveness of this process since they are directly related to the perception of insureds, interactions with public and private institutions, and the social responsibility of the insurance sector itself.

One of the most significant social risks is the underdeveloped insurance culture among the population of Uzbekistan. Insurance is often perceived as something alien or optional, which creates a barrier to the active involvement of citizens in ESG transformation processes. Low awareness of sustainable development principles and their importance for personal and public interests complicates effective decision-making at both the consumer and business levels. This risk is confirmed by insufficient demand for innovative insurance products related to environmental or social responsibility, as well as insufficient public support for initiatives to improve the quality of life and protect the environment. To minimize this risk, it is necessary to actively engage in public education and training, as well as to develop accessible and understandable insurance products that will facilitate the ESG values integration into everyday life.

Uzbekistan also faces the problem of low trust in financial and insurance organizations. Historically established relationships between insureds and insurers can be troubled by mistrust, which is especially vital in the context of the new ESG standards transition. Companies introducing ESG principles face the risk that consumers will perceive their initiatives as marketing strategies aimed only at improving reputation, rather than as real steps to ensure sustainable development. Failure to effectively overcome this social barrier can significantly reduce the ESG transformation effectiveness in the insurance market. It is important for insurance companies to demonstrate genuine changes in their policies and corporate practices, actively communicate, and build trustworthy relationships with clients based on transparency and responsibility.

ESG transformation in the insurance sector should take into account social justice and insurance services accessibility for all population segments. There is significant social inequality in Uzbekistan, and one of the issues is that not all citizens have equal access to insurance services, especially in remote regions. This creates a social risk associated with a possible increase in inequality in access to protection and social security. The implementation of ESG standards in insurance should include strategies aimed at removing barriers such as high prices, limited geographic accessibility, and lack of awareness. Insurance companies should develop products that will be accessible to a wide audience, including the most vulnerable groups, such as low-income groups and residents of rural areas.

At the ESG transformation stage, companies will face the need to include social responsibility in their strategies. Insurance companies that do not take into account the social needs and interests of their clients are at risk of being perceived as organizations focused solely on financial benefit. In conditions of the insurance sector transformation, it is important for companies to focus on such social aspects as local community support, infrastructure development for social groups, and the development of sustainable and ethical products that meet the needs and expectations of the population. Lack of attention to social responsibility can lead to deterioration in the company's image and decreased competitiveness in the market.

The ESG principles' introduction also has an impact on the labor sphere. When implementing sustainable practices in insurance companies, changes may occur in the employment structure and requirements for employee qualifications. This may create risks for those employees who are not ready to adapt to new standards and requirements in the field of corporate social responsibility. In addition, it is necessary to take into account potential social consequences for insurance company personnel, such as increased workload and the need for additional knowledge and skills to work in the context of new ESG standards. To minimize these risks, companies must invest in staff training and development, and they must create conditions for smooth adaptation of employees to changes in corporate culture.

An important aspect of ESG transformation is compliance with the principles of social inclusiveness and justice. In conditions of global challenges and changes, companies will have to integrate these principles into their practices, ensuring equal opportunities for all population groups. In particular, this concerns recruitment policy, equal wages, ensuring working conditions, and creating equal opportunities for women, people with disabilities, and other socially vulnerable groups. Ignoring these aspects can lead to negative social consequences, such as increased social tension, which can in turn affect the stability and reputation of the company.

The social risks of ESG transformation in the insurance market of Uzbekistan constitute a multi-layered problem requiring a comprehensive approach and careful work with all stakeholders. To effectively overcome these risks, it is necessary to establish conditions for increasing trust, improving the accessibility and fairness of insurance services, and developing social strategies aimed at improving the quality of life for citizens and the sustainable development of society as a whole.

The ESG transformation process in the insurance sector poses significant challenges for management practices, as it requires not only the operation of new strategies and principles but also the creation of sustainable instruments for managing the risks faced by insurance companies. Managing these risks is necessary to ensure the effective and long-term implementation of environmental, social, and corporate standards. In the context of this process, several key management risks are highlighted that require careful analysis and development of appropriate strategies to minimize them.

One of the most significant management risks is the possibility of losing customer confidence, which may negatively affect the company's business results. ESG principles' introduction involves not only formal changes in the company's policy but also demonstrating real efforts toward sustainable development. Lack of communication transparency, as well as the absence of consistent actions, may lead to customers perceiving ESG initiatives as a greenwashing exercise, which can in turn undermine the company's reputation and reduce its competitiveness. To effectively manage this risk, it is necessary to ensure a high degree of transparency in reporting, regularly inform clients about the company's achieved results and plans, and implement objective mechanisms for assessing the impact of ESG practices.

Introducing ESG principles into the activities of an insurance company requires fundamental changes in corporate governance. Issues with the integration of environmental, social, and corporate factors into strategic planning, risk management, and financial reporting can lead to insufficient efficiency and even errors in decision-making. An important aspect is the need to improve the internal management structure, including the introduction of specialized positions and units responsible for the implementation of ESG strategies. It is also worth noting the importance of training top management and key employees in implementing and managing ESG practices since the lack of competencies in this area can become a significant barrier to successful transformation.

Significant obstacles to successful ESG transformation include the imperfect nature of the national legislative framework and inconsistencies in existing regulatory mechanisms with international ESG standards. In conditions of rapidly changing legislation and regulations, insurance companies may face uncertainty in the process of adapting their operations to new requirements. This is due to the need to integrate international norms and standards into the national legal system, which, in turn, requires significant effort from companies in terms of monitoring and adjusting their activities in accordance with the changing legislative landscape. It is important for companies to actively cooperate with regulators and participate in the process of developing regulatory legal acts, which will minimize the risks of non-compliance and ensure smoother adaptation to international standards.

The implementation of ESG principles is related to the need for significant financial investments in infrastructure modernization, development of new products and services, and personnel training. In the short term, this may lead to increased costs, which will in turn affect the company's profitability. In addition, there are risks associated with the fact that investments in sustainable technologies and projects may not pay off within the expected timeframe, which will create additional financial problems for the company. To minimize these risks, companies need to develop financial strategies that include not only short-term expenses but also long-term benefits from implementing ESG principles. Forecasting potential financial consequences and diversifying risks play a key role in the successful implementation of ESG transformation.

One of the central aspects of ESG transformation is the development of new products that are focused on environmental, social, and corporate standards. However, the process of developing and implementing such products relates to a number of risks, including uncertainty in demand for new insurance types and difficulties in ensuring compliance with new environmental and social standards. Problems with market demand or a lack of a clear regulatory framework can lead to financial losses and a decrease in consumer confidence. To avoid these risks, it is necessary to conduct in-depth market research and develop products that will meet the real needs of customers and the requirements of regulators.

Data management and reporting are important aspects of implementing ESG strategies. Insurance companies must form a system for collecting and analyzing data that reflects their impact on the environment, society, and corporate practices. However, there are risks related to data inconsistencies, difficulties in standardizing ESG metrics, and insufficient reporting accuracy. Incorrect interpretation or incomplete data can lead to wrong management decisions, as well as issues with reporting to regulators and stakeholders. To minimize this risk, companies need to develop reliable systems for monitoring, collecting, and analyzing data and ensure that they comply with international standards.

ESG transformation requires changes in the company's corporate culture, which may be resisted by employees, especially if they do not understand the importance and necessity of such changes. Issues with adapting personnel to new principles and values, as well as with corporate social responsibility development, can reduce the effectiveness of the ESG initiatives. To overcome this risk, companies need to actively work with personnel, conducting training and motivating them to integrate sustainable practices into the company's daily activities.

Thus, the ESG transformation of the insurance market relates to a multitude of management risks that require a comprehensive approach to their identification, analysis, and minimization. Successful implementation of ESG strategies in the insurance industry is impossible without effective management of these risks, which requires strategic vision, highly qualified personnel, and constant adaptation to changing external and internal conditions.

3.4 Conclusions

1. The evolution of ESG principles in the insurance business is a systemic process of institutionalizing sustainable development in the corporate environment. Historically dating back to the international environmental initiatives of the 1970s, the ESG agenda has undergone transformation from a marginal aspect to an integral element of the strategic management of insurance companies. At the present stage, the principles of environmental sustainability, social responsibility, and effective corporate governance are integrated into core business models, followed by the development of specialized insurance products, increased reporting standards, and operational processes digitalization.

   In the context of Uzbekistan, the ESG transformation of the insurance sector reflects adaptation to global trends through national strategic initiatives, including the "green" economy development and institutional environment strengthening. The introduction of ESG approaches not only helps to increase the resilience of insurance companies to environmental and social risks but also opens up prospects for attracting international investment. Thus, ESG principles become a tool for sustainable growth while also strengthening competitive positions in the context of the insurance market's global transformation.
2. In the context of a transition economy, the ESG transformation of insurers is a strategically important tool for ensuring sustainable development and increasing competitiveness. Its successful implementation requires a comprehensive, multi-level approach, including adaptation to local conditions and international standards, institutional framework development, digitalization, ESG-oriented corporate culture formation, and effective interaction with stakeholders. The key elements of the strategy are environmental responsibility, social inclusiveness, and corporate governance improvement, supported by innovative technologies and sustainable financial instruments. Monitoring and reporting, as well as compliance with regulatory requirements, ensure transparency and strengthen market confidence. The proposed strategy development algorithm contributes to the formation of a sustainable business model for insurers that meets modern challenges and promotes long-term development in transition economies.
3. The ESG transformation of the insurance market in Uzbekistan is a comprehensive and multifaceted process, triggered by the unique climatic, environmental, and social characteristics of the country, as well as the insufficient level of insurance culture and public trust. Successful implementation of the ESG principles requires a systematic approach, including the development and implementation of adaptive risk management strategies, modernization of the regulatory framework, increased transparency and responsibility of insurance companies, and active interaction with society. Effective management of ESG risks is becoming a key factor in ensuring sustainable development and competitiveness of the insurance sector in Uzbekistan in the context of global challenges and growing international requirements.

Chapter 4

Innovative Aspects of ESG Transformation of Insurance Business

4.1 Digital Transformation of the Insurance Business

Digital transformation of the insurance business driven by ESG principles is becoming an important aspect in a transition economy. The digital transformation of the insurance business in the context of this study represents the process of integrating digital technologies into all aspects of the activities of insurance companies, which significantly changes their workflows, client interactions, and service provision. Digital transformation in insurance involves not only technological changes but also a strategic approach to risk management. Using data and analytical tools, insurance companies can offer more personalized solutions, which allows them to reduce risks and increase customer confidence.

In addition, the integration of new insurance products into business processes for large projects opens up opportunities for a more comprehensive approach to insurance, including risk assessment and management at all levels. This creates additional value for both insureds and insurance companies.

The digital transformation of the insurance business in Uzbekistan is a multifaceted process that encompasses technological, organizational, and managerial changes aimed at improving the availability and quality of insurance services. In conditions of the global transition to a digital economy and active government support for the digitalization of the financial sector, Uzbekistan seeks to integrate the latest technologies into the insurance industry to increase competitiveness, improve customer experience, and stimulate economic growth. Let's consider the main directions and achievements of the digital transformation of the insurance industry in Uzbekistan.

Insurers increasingly integrate ESG factors into their strategy and operations, and in the face of growing climate risks, they are taking proactive measures to assess and manage environmental threats. Specific approaches to ensure environmental sustainability include the following:

- The use of digital models that predict climate change and its impacts: This could include creating risk maps based on flood, hurricane, and wildfire data, with insurers using geographic information systems (GIS) to visualize the data and identify high-risk areas.
- The development of sustainability-oriented policies such as "green insurance" provides discounts to customers who use renewable energy or implement environmentally friendly practices.
- IoT devices and sensors can be used to collect information about the state of natural ecosystems, which helps in assessing risks and reducing impacts on nature.

- Forming partnerships with local authorities and NGOs for implementing programs to improve infrastructure and make communities more resilient to climate risks: This could include funding projects to strengthen dams or install early warning systems for natural or man-made disasters.

Social responsibility is becoming an important part of business, and insurance companies can contribute to society through the following ways:

1. Development of specialized products, for example, inclusive insurance or microinsurance, which enables low-income people to access basic insurance services: This could include policies for farm households, private or small businesses, or informal sector workers who are often left without protection.
2. Conducting seminars and online courses on financial literacy and insurance issues to a wide audience: This will help raise awareness of the importance of insurance and the products available.
3. Social programs: Implementing programs aimed at supporting local communities, such as investing in projects aimed at improving health, education, or public safety: This could include funding educational institutions or supporting local health initiatives.

To practically implement ESG principles in the field of corporate governance, insurers:

1. Use digital platforms to provide customers with access to information about the company's performance, which may include interactive dashboards where users can see how the insurer is achieving its ESG goals;
2. Implement risk management systems that take into account ESG factors in assessing financial and operational risks, for example, insurance companies may conduct stress tests to assess the impact of environmental and social factors on their financial performance;
3. Form special ESG committees that monitor implementation of strategies and policies related to sustainable development, which increases the level of responsibility and involvement in ESG issues at the highest management level.

Integrating ESG principles into the insurance business requires a systematic approach and innovative solutions. Insurance companies that actively implement these principles not only respond to the challenges of the modern world but also gain competitive advantages. Sustainable development is becoming not merely a fashionable trend but a necessity that helps attract clients and investors interested in long-term sustainability and social responsibility.

Insurance industry digitalization is an important trend that both contributes to the efficiency of processes and allows companies to better adapt to changing customer needs and market conditions. Let's take a closer look at the key areas related to the digitalization of key technological processes.

1. Shifting the full cycle of interaction with the client online. This includes finding clients, consulting services, accepting insurance applications, calculating the rate under the agreement, drafting and concluding agreements, receiving full or partial payment of the insurance premium, obtaining insurance policies, filing insurance event claims, and settling insurance claims.

Digital customer searches are carried out through the use of digital platforms and marketing tools to attract the target audience and expand the database of potential insureds. This may include contextual advertising, SEO, social networks, and email marketing.

Conducting online consultations with clients via video calls, text chats, or emails allows for flexibility and accessibility of services, as well as increasing the level of interaction with clients. Specialists can not only answer questions but also conduct a detailed analysis of client needs, offer individual solutions, and explain insurance terms. In addition, the use of modern technology allows recording sessions for subsequent analysis and training, as well as storing correspondence to ensure interaction transparency. This creates an atmosphere of trust and helps strengthen relationships with clients.

Accepting applications for insurance is a critical step in the work of insurance companies. The efficiency of this process directly affects customer satisfaction and overall business performance.

Insurance companies such as Allstate[1] and State Farm Insurance[2] offer clients custom platforms where customers can get quotes, fill in applications, and manage policies. Mobile applications provide the ability to submit a claim anytime, anywhere. User platforms often have a simple and intuitive interface, allowing customers to fill out applications without much effort. Simplified forms that suggest what data to enter help to quickly complete the process.

Some companies, such as Lemonade,[3] use AI chatbots to interact with customers. These bots can quickly answer questions, help fill out forms, and even process simple requests. Moreover, chatbots work around the clock, which allows for customer support regardless of the time of day and improves the overall customer experience.

Platforms like DocuSign[4] or Adobe Sign[5] allow customers to sign documents online, simplifying the application process and reducing processing time. These solutions provide a high level of security and compliance with legal requirements, which increases customer confidence.

Uzbekinvest Export-Import Insurance Company JSC (hereinafter referred to as Uzbekinvest) is the apparent leader in digital technologies use in the insurance market of Uzbekistan. It actively implements innovative solutions aimed at improving the efficiency of customer service and data security. The introduction of the Face ID biometric system ensured reliable identification of insureds, which significantly increased the security level of interactions with clients. The use of biometric data minimized the likelihood of fraud, ensuring reliability and the protection of personal information. Thanks to the introduction of the Face ID biometric system (Fig. 4.1), the time for reissuing policies has been reduced from 7–8 minutes to 20–30 seconds, which improves customer experience and increases the efficiency of the company. More than 73% of customers now use Face ID to reissue policies, which confirms the popularity of the system.

---

[1] https://www.allstate.com/.

[2] https://www.statefarm.com/.

[3] https://www.lemonade.com/.

[4] https://www.docusign.com/.

[5] https://www.adobe.com/sign.html.

In January 2024, Uzbekinvest, together with its international partner, Glow Bite, launched Talys.SDE – a real-time pre-insurance check scoring system.

Currently, more than 87% of agreements are checked through this system.

In May 2024, the company began implementing Uzbekinvest Reinsurance Automation Platform to improve the underwriting process in reinsurance. It is expected to process 90% of facultative enquiries from the international market, which will at least double the speed of the underwriting process.

The company plans to introduce the corporate data warehouse and business analytics for automating management decisions by the end of 2024, the implementation of which will allow it to:

1. conduct business process analysis in real time,
2. increase efficiency and improve the quality of business analysts,
3. optimize product management costs,
4. use the capabilities of AI to study historical retrospectives and forecast expected trends.

Automation of the application process reduces the time required for processing, allowing customers to receive the protection they need faster. Electronic forms and automated processes reduce errors due to manual data entry, increasing the accuracy and reliability of information. Simplified processes and accessibility of services contribute to increased customer satisfaction and brand loyalty.

Automating the application process for signing insurance agreements using custom platforms and mobile applications is an important step toward the digital transformation of insurance companies. This not only improves the customer experience but also allows companies to manage resources efficiently, increasing their competitiveness in the market. It is important to continue developing these technologies to adapt to changing customer requirements and provide a high service level.

The use of automated calculators and online systems allows customers to independently and quickly calculate the cost of insurance services. Such tools take into account various parameters such as insurance type, type of production, client age, health status, and other individual characteristics. This makes the process of calculating the insurance premium more transparent and convenient. In addition, automated systems can offer recommendations for tariff optimization and provide options that meet the client's needs. This way, clients can easily compare offers and make informed decisions.

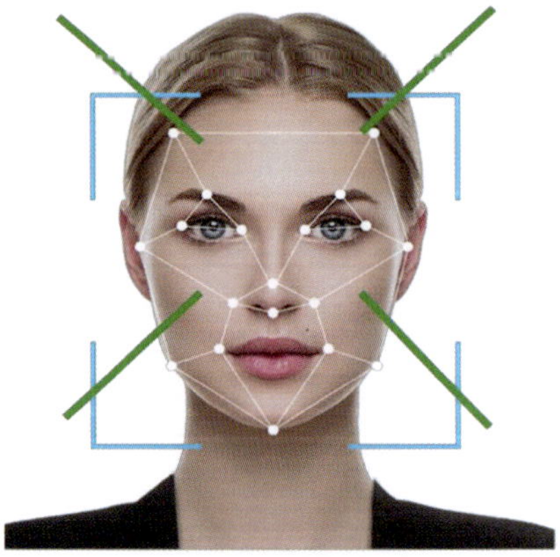

Fig. 4.1. Face ID system reference points.

The use of electronic documents and digital signatures to make and sign agreements ensures fast and secure document management, minimizing paperwork. Clients can receive insurance agreements by email, make necessary changes, and sign them online, which significantly speeds up the procedure. Electronic documents can also be automatically integrated into accounting and management systems, ensuring reliable storage and easy access to information. This approach increases convenience for clients and reduces the risk of errors due to manual data entry. Ultimately, this allows for faster conclusion of agreements and improved overall customer experience.

Customers can easily and quickly pay their insurance premiums using their bank cards, e-wallets, or mobile apps, making the process simpler and more convenient. Such solutions ensure transaction security and allow for real-time payment tracking. In addition, integration with automated accounting systems allows for instant payment status updates, minimizing the risk of misunderstandings and delays. This approach also allows customers to set up automatic payments, eliminating the need to constantly monitor payment deadlines and improving financial planning.

Using online forms to submit claims and required documents greatly simplifies the insurance claims process. Such forms allow users to fill in information about the insurance claim in a convenient format, attach the necessary documents, and submit all materials directly via the Internet. This speeds up claims processing and reduces the number of errors due to manual data entry. Online systems can also include automated notifications about the claim status, which ensures process transparency and allows customers to stay informed. In addition, access to data in electronic form makes it easier for companies to analyze and manage insurance claims, increasing overall efficiency.

Moreover, automated systems can offer customers payment options and notify them of the necessary actions, which makes the process more transparent and understandable. This approach not only increases customer satisfaction but also helps build trust in the company.

2. Robotic Process Automation (RPA) is a technology that enables the automation of routine and repetitive tasks using "robots" that imitate human actions in various applications. In the insurance industry, RPA is increasingly used to raise efficiency and reduce time spent on routine processes. This allows employees to focus on more complex tasks that require analytical thinking and creativity. As a result, management decisions become more effective and informed, which helps raise the company's competitiveness in the market.

   RPA is a powerful tool for increasing efficiency and reducing time costs in the insurance industry. Implementing RPA allows companies to focus on strategic tasks, improve customer experience, and reduce operational costs. However, successful implementation requires careful attention to technology integration and change management.

   The company Allianz introduced RPA to automate claims processing and customer engagement.[6] This has significantly improved processing times for enquiries and increased customer satisfaction. AXA uses RPA to automate routine processes such as collecting customer data and updating information in systems. This helped reduce operating costs and improve service quality. AIG uses RPA to automate financial

[6]https://www.blueprism.com/resources/case-studies/allianz-builds-a-future-ready-business-with-intelligent-automation/.

operations, including invoice and payment processing.[7] This resulted in a significant reduction in the time required to complete these tasks.

3. Chatbot technologies allow you to quickly and effectively answer the most frequently asked questions of customers. Chatbots work around the clock, providing prompt information without the need to wait for a response from a company employee. This significantly saves time for both insurers and insureds, improving the overall interaction experience. Chatbots can help customers get answers to questions about policies, insurance terms, claims procedures, and more. They can also direct users to the right resources or specialists for more complex queries. Automating these processes not only speeds up interactions but also frees up employees to perform more complex tasks, improving the overall efficiency of the insurer.
4. Data collection and processing from telematic devices (IoT) allow insurers to obtain a wide range of indicators for risk assessment. Remote data collection from telematic devices, such as GPS devices, sensors, and other IoT devices, provides valuable information about customer behavior, their habits, and conditions of use of the insured object.

   With these data, insurers can more accurately assess risks, identify potential threats, and tailor their proposals to individual customer needs. For example, in auto insurance, driving, speed, and frequency data can be used to calculate fairer rates. In addition, this information can help develop personalized insurance programs, which increases customer satisfaction and helps form long-term relationships.
5. Technologies with artificial intelligence (AI) elements, based on big data analysis and effective analytics, enable insurance companies to make informed decisions and optimize processes. With the help of deep learning and machine learning, AI can perform tasks such as assessing customer risks, determining fraud likelihood, and predicting potential financial losses.

   AI analyzes a variety of data, including insurance claim histories, behavioral patterns, and external factors, allowing for more accurate risk assessments. This not only improves the rate selection process but also helps identify suspicious activity and prevent fraudulent schemes. As a result, the use of AI-enabled technologies helps to increase the efficiency of insurance companies, reduce losses, and improve customer service.
6. Blockchain technologies provide reliable solutions for checking clients' personal data and verifying the parameters of actions on insurance objects, both when issuing policies and in the process of settling insurance claims.

   Blockchain provides transparency and security of data storage, which helps to minimize the risk of fraud and increase trust between insurers and clients. All transactions are recorded in an unchangeable registry, which makes them available for verification and audit at any time. This significantly simplifies the process of data exchange between different parties, reducing the time for processing requests and increasing interaction efficiency. As a result, the use of blockchain in insurance helps to improve service quality and increase the level of customer satisfaction.
7. Big Data allows you to analyze huge amounts of data and many factors that influence the risks and unprofitability of transactions. With the ability to process and analyze information in real time, insurers can make more informed decisions and quickly adapt to changing market conditions.

   The use of Big Data makes everyday business processes more efficient and cost-effective, reducing the time for processing information and minimizing costs.

[7] https://aigautomation.co.uk/.

In addition, data analysis allows insurers to individualize the terms of insurance offers, develop personalized rates and offers, which increases customer satisfaction and strengthens their loyalty. As a result, the implementation of Big Data technologies contributes not only to improving operational efficiency but also to increasing the competitiveness of insurance companies in the market.

Significant disadvantages of using digital technologies in insurance include the following:

- **Shortage of qualified personnel with necessary skills to work with new technologies:** This can slow down the implementation of digital solutions and reduce their effectiveness.
- **Long-term return on investment:** Investing in digitalization requires significant resources and time to achieve results, which can take 5–10 years, making such investments less attractive for companies with a short-term perspective.
- **The risk of disappointment in traditional insurance:** Simplified technological processes could lead to a decrease in trust in traditional insurance companies, contributing to the revival of archaic forms of insurance. This could result in mutual insurance schemes or p2p insurance, in which groups of people create funds for payments without the participation of insurance companies.
- **Insufficient development of legislative regulation:** The introduction of digital technologies in insurance often outpaces legislative developments, which can create legal uncertainties and prevent new solutions from being fully exploited.

The advantages of using digital technologies in insurance include the following:

- **Reducing the number of errors:** Automation of processes minimizes the influence of the "human factor", which leads to fewer errors and increased overall reliability of operations.
- **Growth of the information volume:** Access to more data on the insured and the insurance object allows for a more accurate and individual risk assessment.
- **Customer-centricity:** Digital technologies allow for personalized offers, which gives insureds with a positive history and low risks the opportunity to receive more favorable rates.
- **Service time reduction:** Digitalization of processes significantly speeds up service time, allowing customers to receive answers and solutions faster, improving the overall customer experience and increasing satisfaction.

The transformation of the insurance industry in a digital economy opens up new horizons for businesses. The expansion of electronic insurance and online sales channels improves the availability and convenience of services for customers. The introduction of digital technologies such as AI and blockchain facilitates the automation of processes, accelerates the processing of applications, and reduces the fraud risk.

These changes help insurance companies remain competitive in a global market where innovation plays a key role. In addition, digitalization increases the transparency and efficiency of financial systems, which in turn contributes to insurance market development.

Thus, the integration of digital technologies into insurance not only improves the quality of services but also builds a safer and more adaptive ecosystem for all participants.

Insurance digitalization under ESG transformation opens up new opportunities for the development of insurance companies. It not only helps them meet modern requirements but also contributes to the creation of more sustainable and responsible business models. This is becoming an important factor in attracting customers and investors who increasingly value sustainable development and social responsibility.

Digitalization of the insurance industry is an important and integral process that has a significant impact on the development of insurance companies, increasing their operational efficiency and improving the quality of customer service. Progress in digital technologies, such as AI, Big Data, blockchain, and mobile platforms, is shaping a new paradigm for the functioning of insurance organizations. In this context, it is appropriate to consider the features of digitalization of the insurance business both internationally and in Uzbekistan, taking into account current achievements and challenges (Table 4.1).

The insurance business digitalization on a global scale continues to develop rapidly, introducing advanced technologies, as mentioned above. In countries with highly developed insurance markets, this process is not only a requirement of the times but also a necessity to increase competitiveness and improve customer service quality.

In Uzbekistan, the digitalization of the insurance industry is at an early stage, but there is a growing interest in the introduction of modern technologies. At the moment, the country is developing key regulations and establishing conditions for further development of digital services in insurance. The prospects for growth in this sector are significant, but for a full transition to digital platforms, it is necessary to continue efforts to improve the regulatory framework, introduce innovative technologies, and increase the level of digital literacy among market participants.

The digitalization of the insurance market in Uzbekistan is a complex process that includes the integration of modern technologies, infrastructure development, increasing the digital literacy level of the population, and the creation of a favorable institutional environment. Given the global trends of economic digitalization, the need for effective and accessible online services, including insurance, is growing. Uzbekistan has seen an increase in the number of Internet and mobile device users, which creates favorable conditions for the transition to digital platforms. A mathematical model can help in predicting consumer behavior and their preferences in choosing insurance products and optimizing offers to increase competitiveness in the market.

To form a mathematical model, it is important to take into account both exogenous and endogenous factors influencing the digitalization development.

The objectives of the mathematical model are as follows:

- assessment of the current digitalization level of the insurance market;
- forecasting the digitalization dynamics depending on key factors;
- optimization of investment and organizational decisions to accelerate digital transformation.

The mathematical model is based on a number of parameters characterizing various digitalization aspects.

Key variables include the following:

- $S(t)$: total volume of the insurance market (UZS, USD);
- $S_{digital}(t)$: the volume of the digital segment of the insurance market (UZS, USD);
- $D(t)$: digitalization degree of the market ($0 \leq D(t) \leq 1$).

Table 4.1. Comparative table of insurance business digitalization in Uzbekistan and abroad.

No.	Criteria	World Experience	Uzbekistan Experience
1.	Level of industry digitalization	Leading countries (the US, the UK, Germany, and China) are actively using AI, big data, blockchain, and online sales and service platforms. The implementation of smart contracts and process automation is becoming the standard.	In Uzbekistan, the process of the insurance sector digitalization is at an early stage. Online services are developing, but they are still limited to basic functions.
2.	Digital sales and service channels	Online platforms for selling policies, chatbots for customer service, automated systems for filing claims and consultations are widely used. Product comparison platforms are being actively implemented.	In Uzbekistan, online insurance is just beginning to develop. Some companies offer policies online, but the traditional offline format of service is mostly preserved.
3.	Use of artificial intelligence and big data	AI and big data are actively used to analyze customer behavior, assess risks, create personalized offers, and settle claims. AI helps process and analyze large data volumes.	In Uzbekistan, the use of AI is limited, data analysis technologies are at an early stage. AI is mainly used in CRM systems for customer base management.
4.	Blockchain and data protection	Blockchain is used to create smart agreements, increase transparency, speed up transactions, and ensure data security. Countries are actively developing regulations to protect customer data.	In Uzbekistan, blockchain technologies are practically not used in insurance. The possibilities of using them in the financial sector are being discussed, but practical implementation is still limited.
5.	Regulatory initiatives	Countries with high digitalization have developed clear regulations governing the use of digital technologies, including data protection, electronic signature, and cyber insurance.	In Uzbekistan, legislative initiatives in the field of insurance digitalization are just beginning to develop. In 2020, regulations were introduced for the use of electronic signatures and remote conclusion of agreements.
6.	Electronic policies and document flow	Electronic policies and document flow automation are widespread. electronic signatures, systems for automatic verification, and policies approval are standard.	In Uzbekistan, electronic policies in voluntary insurance are just beginning to be implemented. Most processes are still executed on paper.

(*Continued*)

Table 4.1. *(Continued)*

No.	Criteria	World Experience	Uzbekistan Experience
7.	Using technology to prevent fraud	AI-based systems are being developed to prevent fraud, analyze anomalies in customer behavior and in the claims settlement process.	In Uzbekistan, technologies for preventing insurance fraud are just beginning to be implemented. Systems for protecting against fraud at a mass level have not been developed.
8.	Mobile applications and services	In highly digitalized countries, almost all insurance companies offer mobile applications for selling policies, filing claims, and servicing customers.	In Uzbekistan, mobile applications are just beginning to develop. Basic functions are currently available, such as calculating the policy cost, processing documents, and payment.
9.	Innovative insurance products	Introducing new products such as microinsurance, usage-based insurance, and insurance through platforms (e.g. Uber or Airbnb).	In Uzbekistan, innovative products are still limited to traditional insurance types, such as auto and health insurance. Products that use new technologies are rare.
10.	Education and advanced training	In developed countries, online courses and education programs on digital technologies in insurance are actively developing. Professional training covers a wide range of skills.	In Uzbekistan, specialized programs and courses on digital technologies in insurance are just beginning to appear. Professional training in this area is not yet developed.

Digitalization factors:

- ***I(t)***: Internet penetration index ($0 \leq I(t) \leq 1$);
- ***P(t)***: the level of insurance services penetration among the population ($0 \leq P(t) \leq 1$);
- ***C(t)***: level of trust in digital platforms ($0 \leq C(t) \leq 1$);
- ***R(t)***: investments in the insurance market digital infrastructure (UZS, USD);
- ***L(t)***: index of legislative support for digitalization ($0 \leq L(t) \leq 1$);
- ***U(t)***: digital literacy level of the population ($0 \leq U(t) \leq 1$);
- ***G(t)***: macroeconomic conditions (e.g. GDP per capita, UZS, USD). Additional parameters:
  $T_{\text{infra}}(t)$ target level of the Internet infrastructure penetration.
  $E_{\text{edu}}(t)$ intensity of digitalization educational campaigns.

Digital market size:

$$S_{\text{digital}}(t) = S(t) \cdot D(t),$$

where ***D(t)*** is a key digitalization indicator, depending on many factors.

The digitalization degree ***D(t)*** is described through a regression model:

$$D(t) = \alpha_1 I(t) + \alpha_2 P(t) + \alpha_3 C(t) + \alpha_4 R(t) + \alpha_5 L(t) + \alpha_6 U(t) + \alpha_7 G(t) + \varepsilon,$$

where α_i denote weights reflecting each factor's significance and ε is the random error.

Dynamic component: a system of differential equations is used to predict the factors of the model:

- Internet technologies penetration:

$$\frac{dI(t)}{dt} = \beta_1 (T_{\text{infra}}(t) - I(t)),$$

where β_1 is the speed of the Internet infrastructure development;

- penetration of insurance services:

$$\frac{dP(t)}{dt} = \beta_2 (E_{\text{edu}}(t) + D(t) - P(t)),$$

where β_2 is the coefficient of digitalization efficiency for insurance penetration growth;

- investments:

$$\frac{dR(t)}{dt} = \beta_3 (G(t) - R(t)),$$

where β_3 is the coefficient of investment attraction with a growing economy.

The model is aimed at maximizing the digital segment of the insurance market $S_{\text{digital}}(t)$:

$$\max S_{\text{digital}}(t),$$

subject to the restriction:

$$0 \leq D(t) \leq 1 \text{ and } R(t) \leq B(t),$$

where $\boldsymbol{B(t)}$ is the budgetary constraints on digitalization.

Various scenarios are used for the analysis:

1. Optimistic: High investment level, active legislative support, and rapid growth of Internet infrastructure ($\boldsymbol{T_{infra}(t)} \rightarrow 1$).
2. Basic: Moderate digitalization pace with gradual insurance penetration growth.
3. Pessimistic: Insufficient investment and weak institutional support.

The developed model allows us to:

- identify key digitalization drivers and barriers;
- justify strategies for attracting investment in digital infrastructure;
- develop measures to increase trust in digital platforms among the population;
- to assess the impact of educational and advertising campaigns on digitalization acceleration.

The mathematical model for the digitalization of the insurance market in Uzbekistan integrates key aspects of economic, technological, and institutional development. The use of this model can significantly improve the efficiency of planning and implementation of digital transformation programs in the insurance sector.

Digitalization of the insurance market in Uzbekistan is an important step in increasing its competitiveness, improving customer service quality, and increasing insurance companies' efficiency. The mathematical model becomes a necessary tool for optimizing and automating processes, improving risk assessment, forecasting demand, and developing new products. This contributes to both the growth of the country's economy as a whole and increasing the reliability and sustainability of the insurance industry.

4.2 Inclusive Priorities for the Insurance Business Development

In recent years, attention to ESG principles has become an important aspect of insurance companies' strategies. Inclusive insurance, in turn, provides access to insurance services for various population segments, including private and small businesses. This interaction is of great importance for the formation of a sustainable and responsible insurance market.

At the beginning of our study, we define the concept of inclusive insurance. Using this concept, we adopt a broader approach aimed at ensuring access to insurance services for all segments of the population and business entities, including groups that traditionally remain outside the scope of insurance.

The main categories of inclusive insurance are:

- customer-centricity,
- availability,
- technological capability,
- educational initiatives,
- social responsibility.

Customer-centricity, i.e. focusing on the needs and interests of customers, is one of the key aspects of inclusive insurance. This approach implies that insurance products and services are developed taking into account the opinions and experiences of users, which allows them to more effectively meet their needs and increase their satisfaction level.

Active use of various methods to collect customer feedback, such as surveys, interviews, focus groups, and feedback analysis, helps to identify the real needs and expectations of users, as well as their experience with products and services.

Based on the information collected, insurance companies can tailor their offers. This could include changes to policy terms, flexibility in payments, additional services, or a simplified application process.

The essential aspect of customer-centricity is the application of a personalized approach to each client and the use of data and analytics to develop individual offers that correspond to the specific life circumstances and preferences of the client.

Customer education and support are important components of customer-centricity, aimed at ensuring understanding and informed choice of insurance products. This includes several key areas:

- Development of simple and understandable information materials, such as brochures, video tutorials, and infographics that explain basic insurance concepts, policy terms and the claims process: These materials should be tailored to different target audiences, taking into account the financial literacy level and experience of customers.
- Holding regular online and offline events, where experts can share knowledge and answer customer questions: Webinars can cover topics such as insurance basics, policy selection tips, and real-life case studies.
- Providing clients with the opportunity to receive individual consultations with insurance experts: This can be done through hotlines, online chats, or office meetings, allowing customers to ask questions and get clarification on specific situations.
- Development of interactive platforms and mobile applications allowing customers to research insurance products and services on their own: This may include premium calculators, scenario simulators or FAQs.
- Development of mentoring programs where more experienced users can share their experiences and help newcomers understand insurance issues: This can be especially useful for vulnerable groups who may be less knowledgeable about insurance products.
- Keeping customers informed about changes in insurance products and legislation by providing regular updates via email or in-app notifications.
- Development of mechanisms for collecting feedback on the learning process and support to continually improve programs and materials based on customer needs.

Customer-centricity not only helps to increase trust and loyalty from customers but also improves the overall efficiency of insurance services. Understanding customer needs and tailoring products to their needs allows insurance companies to stand out in a competitive market, enhancing their reputation and attracting new customers. Ultimately, this approach helps to create a more sustainable and inclusive insurance system, where the interests and needs of customers are at the center of attention.

Inclusive insurance aims to make insurance products accessible to all population segments, including low-income workers, farmers, and people living in remote areas, as well as private and small business entities, for any reason or another, who do not have access to traditional insurance services.

The main directions of inclusive insurance development in Uzbekistan are presented in Table 4.2.

Table 4.2. Main directions of inclusive insurance development in Uzbekistan.

Development Direction	Target Group	Measures	Expected Effects	Examples/Indicators
1. Microinsurance	Small businesses, farmers, and self-employed individuals	• Development of affordable tariffs • Partnership with microfinance organizations • Digital registration platforms	• Increased insurance coverage in rural areas • Reduced risks for small businesses	• Number of policies issued • % of rural clients in the portfolio
2. Social insurance	Vulnerable groups (disabled people, retirees, and large families)	• Preferential programs with state support • Simplified underwriting • Informing through social services	• Increasing financial protection for socially vulnerable groups • Reducing poverty	• Number of preferential policies • Regional cover
3. Women's insurance	Women (entrepreneurs and mothers)	• Special products (insurance of pregnancy, women's business) • Financial literacy training	• Increasing the share of female clients • Supporting women's entrepreneurship	• % of women in the insurance portfolio • Number of trained individuals
4. Information inclusion	Youth, especially in remote regions	• Mobile applications with simple interface • Online consultations • Cashless payments	• Attracting young audience • Accessibility in remote areas	• Number of app downloads • % of online sales
5. Agricultural insurance	Farmers and agricultural workers	• Weather index products • Crop insurance • Government subsidies	• Stabilization of farmers' incomes • Increasing the agro-industrial complex sustainability	• Volume of insured crops • Number of indemnities for agricultural risks
6. Education programs	Population (all groups)	• Financial literacy courses • Webinars on the importance of insurance • School programs	• Insurance culture growth • Increase in demand for products	• Number of program participants • Level of awareness (surveys)

Inclusive insurance accessibility implies the formation of conditions under which various population groups, as well as private and small business entities, can easily and without barriers receive insurance services. This includes both geographical and financial accessibility, as well as mental accessibility.

Geographical accessibility is ensured by the fact that insurance companies provide inclusive insurance coverage not only for large cities but also for rural and remote areas, while striving to provide the necessary information to insureds in accessible languages, using simple and understandable terms.

Financial accessibility of insurance premiums for vulnerable population groups is achieved through a comprehensive approach to developing tariffs that take into account the income level of clients. This allows for the development of more flexible and tailored offers that correspond to the financial capabilities of different population categories. For example, tariffs can vary depending on income, providing an opportunity to choose the most suitable option.

In addition, the introduction of subsidies and financial support plays a key role in reducing barriers to access to inclusive insurance. Government programs or private initiatives can offer financial assistance to cover part of the insurance premium, which is especially important for low-income families. Such measures help expand insurance coverage, allowing more people to receive protection against risks.

Moreover, insurance companies can introduce educational programs to help vulnerable groups better understand the insurance benefits and the different types of policies. This, in turn, will increase trust in insurance services and encourage their use.

Ultimately, the integration of adaptive tariffs and financial support not only improves insurance affordability but also contributes to a more sustainable and inclusive insurance system, which ultimately benefits society as a whole.

Mental accessibility of insurance refers not only to the physical ability to obtain insurance services but also to the level of understanding, awareness, and confidence of customers in these products. This is a key aspect, especially for vulnerable population groups who may face barriers to using insurance services.

An important aspect is the standardization of agreements and insurance conditions to reduce the complexity of choice; insurance products should be intuitive and easy to explain.

Mental health coverage accessibility plays a key role in ensuring broad access to insurance services. Insurance companies that actively work on simplifying their products, educational initiatives, and eliminating social and cultural barriers can significantly increase customer trust and engagement. This will not only improve the financial stability of vulnerable groups but also increase overall satisfaction with insurance services.

Using digital technologies to improve access to insurance products and services, such as mobile apps and online platforms, can greatly simplify the interaction of insureds (insured persons) with insurance companies.

Technological ability in inclusive insurance plays a key role in expanding access to insurance products and services, improving service quality, and making insurance processes easier to understand.

Developing intuitive interfaces for purchasing, managing, and filing claims under insurance policies greatly simplifies customer interactions, allowing users to access the services they need anytime, anywhere.

Transition to electronic document flow reduces bureaucratic barriers, eliminates the need for paperwork, and speeds up the process of issuing policies. Clients can sign documents in a few clicks, saving time and effort.

Modern technologies allow us to analyze data about clients and their behavior, which helps to more accurately predict the likelihood of insurance events. This, in turn, leads to fairer and more tailored rates for different population groups. Analysis of client needs allows us to develop individual insurance products that better meet specific conditions and risks.

Introducing chatbots to provide advice and answers to frequently asked questions significantly reduces waiting times and improves customer experience. This allows customers to quickly get the information they need without having to wait for an operator to respond. Using analytics to understand customer preferences and needs helps insurance companies tailor their products. This may include changes to insurance terms, adding new services, or improving existing ones.

The integration of new technologies not only increases the efficiency of processes but also contributes to the formation of a more transparent and sustainable insurance system. This is important for increasing customer trust and ensuring their protection. The integration of technologies allows for the development of more personalized products that better meet the needs of customers and help them manage their risks.

Technology in inclusive insurance helps develop accessible and understandable insurance products, making them more attractive to potential insureds. The use of modern technologies improves service quality, reduces the time required to complete applications, and increases the level of trust in insurance companies. Innovations in this area open up new opportunities for adapting insurance to the needs of different population groups, ensuring financial security and sustainability.

Educational initiatives in inclusive insurance play a crucial role in increasing financial literacy and awareness among vulnerable groups. These initiatives help people better understand their rights and opportunities, which contributes to increasing the number of insured people and improving their financial resilience. By focusing on education, insurance companies can form more equitable and accessible insurance systems that meet the needs of all segments of society.

Specialized programs, accessible courses, and interactive learning formats contribute to a more equitable and accessible insurance system. By investing in education, insurance companies can help people better understand their rights and opportunities, which will ultimately lead to an increase in the number of insured people and improved financial stability of society as a whole.

Social media is a powerful tool for spreading information about insurance and engaging audiences in educational programs. Sharing real customer stories, developing educational content, and engaging users in active discussions helps raise awareness of insurance and demonstrates its value. This not only helps create a more informed society but also improves the relationship between insurance companies and customers, creating an atmosphere of trust and support.

Social responsibility in inclusive insurance covers a wide range of initiatives aimed at improving access to insurance products, supporting vulnerable groups, and promoting sustainable development of society. Insurance companies that take on social responsibility contribute to improving the quality of life of people; they also create a more sustainable and fair economic system. Thus, the introduction of social initiatives into the business model of insurance companies becomes an important factor in their success and fosters trust from customers.

Inclusive insurance is an important step toward forming a fairer and more accessible insurance system that meets the needs of all segments of society. Customer centricity, availability, technological capability, educational initiatives, and social responsibility are some of the key features that help to increase the level of financial literacy and confidence of clients, creating conditions for sustainable development and trust in insurance companies. By investing in these aspects, insurance companies not only improve the quality of life of their clients but also contribute to the creation of a more sustainable economic system as a whole.

The interaction of inclusive insurance and ESG principles in the insurance market represents a strategic opportunity for insurers. This interaction not only helps expand access to insurance services but also increases the financial stability of insureds and increases their social significance. Insurers that actively implement these principles can improve their reputation and competitiveness while making a significant contribution to the formation of a more equitable and sustainable society.

Inclusive priorities for the insurance business development in Uzbekistan are aimed at creating conditions that allow for expanded access to insurance services for various categories of the population and economic entities, including socially vulnerable groups, small and medium businesses, rural entrepreneurs, and residents of remote regions. Under the conditions of a national economic transformation aimed at increasing sustainability and social equality, inclusive insurance becomes an integral part of the state's socio-economic policy. In this regard, inclusive insurance acts not only as a financial protection mechanism but also as a tool for social progress that helps improve financial literacy, strengthen social stability, and stimulate entrepreneurial activity.

Let us consider the main inclusive priorities for the insurance business development in Uzbekistan, their impact on the social and economic structure of society, and the mechanisms and instruments aimed at implementing these priorities:

1. Ensuring insurance accessibility for socially vulnerable people groups.

   The inclusive insurance availability is determined primarily by the size of the insurance rate and the sum insured. The calculation of the tariff rate for inclusive insurance is determined by the gross rate. The gross rate consists of the net rate to ensure current insurance indemnities under insurance agreements and the loading to cover the costs of conducting insurance and forming reserves for preventive measures. The tariff rate is calculated for one insurance year as a percentage of the sum insured (Figure 4.2).

   Net rate $\boldsymbol{T}_{\text{net}}$ consists of two parts – the basic part $\boldsymbol{T}_{\text{netb}}$ and risk premium $\boldsymbol{T}_{\text{netr}}$:

$$T_{\text{net}} = T_{\text{netb}} + T_{\text{netr}}.$$

   The basic part of the net rate $\boldsymbol{T}_{\text{netb}}$ is calculated using the formula

$$T_{\text{netb}} = 100\% \cdot \frac{sp}{s} \cdot q,$$

where:

$\boldsymbol{S}_p$ – average indemnity payment under one insurance agreement in the case of the insurance event;

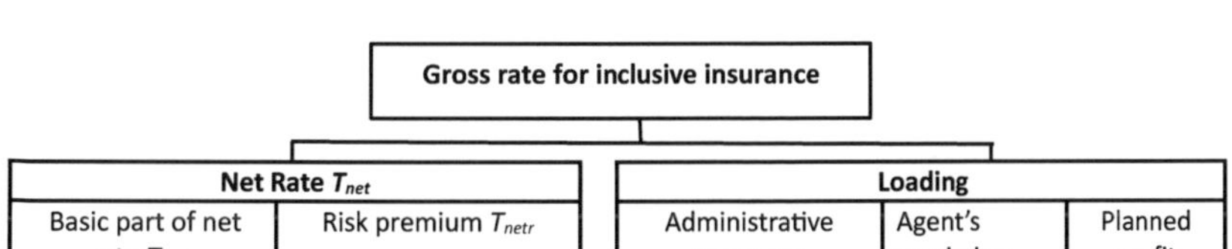

Fig. 4.2. Gross rate structure for inclusive insurance.

S – the average sum insured under one insurance agreement;

q – the probability of occurrence of the insurance event under one insurance agreement.

The probability of occurrence of the insurance event under one insurance agreement ***q*** is determined by

$$q = \frac{M}{N},$$

where ***M*** is the number of insurance cases in *N* contracts and ***N*** is the total number of insurance agreements concluded within some period of time in the past.

In turn, the average sum insured under one insurance agreement ***S*** is determined by

$$S = \frac{\sum_{i=1}^{N} S_i}{N},$$

where S_i is the sum insured upon conclusion of insurance agreement ***i***, ***i*** = 1, 2, 3,…, *N*.

Average indemnity payment under one insurance agreement upon occurrence of insurance event ***Sp:***

$$Sp = \frac{\sum_{i=1}^{N} Spk}{M},$$

where S_{pk} is the insurance indemnity in the case of insurance case ***k***, ***k*** = 1, 2, 3,… *M*.

Risk premium T_{netr} for each case can be determined as

$$T_{\text{netr}} = T_{\text{netb}} \cdot \alpha(\gamma) \sqrt{\frac{1}{nq}} \cdot \left\{ 1 - q + \left(\frac{Rp}{Sp} \right)^2 \right\},$$

where:

α(γ) – coefficient depending on the security guarantee *γ* and determined from the following table:

γ	0.84	0.9	0.95	0.98	0.9986
α(γ)	1	1.3	1.645	2	3

R_p – standard deviation of S_{pk}, ***k*** = 1, 2, 3, … *M*.

If statistical data are available, the dispersion of insurance indemnities can be estimated:

$$R_p^2 = \frac{1}{M-1} \sum_{K=1}^{M} (S_{pk} - S_p)^2 = \frac{1}{M-1} \sum_{K=1}^{M} S_{pk^2} - \frac{M}{M-1} S_{p^2}.$$

In the absence of data on the R_p size, the surcharge T_{netr} is calculated using the formula

$$T_{\text{netr}} = 1{,}2 \cdot T_{\text{netb}} \cdot \alpha(\gamma) \sqrt{\frac{1-q}{nq}},$$

where ***n*** is the expected number of agreements,

Risk premium T_{netr} across the total insurance portfolio may be defined as follows:

$$T_{netr} = T_{netb} \cdot \alpha(\gamma) \cdot \mu,$$

where μ is the coefficient of variation of insurance indemnity payment, corresponding to the ratio of the standard deviation to the expected insurance indemnity payments.

In the absence of statistical data, the value μ may be defined as follows:

$$\mu = 1{,}2\sqrt{\frac{\sum_{j=1}^{m} S_{Bj}^2 \cdot n_j \cdot q_j \left(1 - q_j\right)}{\sum_{j=1}^{m} S_{Bj}^2 \cdot n_j \cdot q_j}}.$$

Based on the obtained value of the net rate T_{net}, gross value rate in inclusive insurance is determined by

$$T_{br} = \frac{T_{net}}{100 - f'}$$

where f is the share of the loading in the total tariff rate.

As a rule, the value of f is determined by the amount of expenses on business management and agent fees. Given the commercial nature of inclusive insurance, the amount of planned profit usually does not exceed 5%. Therefore, with the recommended share of the loading in the total tariff rate of 25%, the share of business management and agent fees accounts for 20%.

To calculate the required sum insured in the context of ensuring the financial stability of the insurer, we use an integral approach, in which the formula for calculating the required sum insured, S, can be written as an integral:

$$S = \int_0^T \frac{L(t) \cdot P(t)}{(1+r)^t} d(t),$$

where S is the sum insured that must be established to ensure payment of all potential losses; $L(t)$ is a function that describes the value of losses that the insurer will have to cover at time t; $P(t)$ is the probability function of the insurance event occurrence at time t; r is the discount rate, which takes into account the time value of money; and T is the final period of time during which the insurer undertakes to provide insurance coverage.

The loss value $L(t)$ at time t is the expected amount that the insurer must pay if the insurance event occurs at that time. This amount may depend on many factors, such as the following:

Inflation: The value of losses may increase over time. For example, the value of property or medical services may increase.
Increasing risks: The probability of loss occurrence and its magnitude may increase over time, for example due to deterioration of the insured property, aging of the insured object, or an increase in the age of the insured person.

The function $L(t)$ can be represented as any time function that reflects the change in the value of losses, for example:

$$L(t) = L_0 \cdot e^{\delta t},$$

where L_0 is the initial value of losses at time t and δ is a coefficient reflecting the growth rate of losses (for example, inflation).

The probability of the insurance event occurrence *P(t)* may change over time depending on various factors:

The service life of the object: The probability of occurrence increases with the service life of the object.
Condition of the insured object: For property insurance, the probability of the property damage may increase with deterioration of its condition or changes in operating conditions.

The function *P(t)* can be represented as a time function reflecting changes in the probability of event occurrence. For example:

$$P(t) = P_0 \cdot e^{\lambda t},$$

where P_0 is the initial probability of the event occurrence and λ is a coefficient reflecting the rate of change in probability.

The discount rate r is used to take into account the time value of money. Due to inflation and interest rate changes, money received or paid in the future has a lower value than the money at the insurer's disposal today.

The time period T is defined as the insurance policy duration. The integral sums up all the payments that the insurer will have to make over this entire period of time. The period T may vary depending on the terms of the agreement.

The integral in this model is the sum of all the insurer's obligations that will arise over time from 0 to T. For each time interval t, the amount of the sum insured, discounted to the current time, is calculated, and this amount is integrated over the entire time interval.

Ensuring inclusive access to insurance for socially vulnerable groups, including low-income families, people with disabilities, and senior citizens, is a priority. These groups are typically at increased risk of financial instability and vulnerability in the case of insurance events. Affordable health and life insurance can provide these population segments with basic financial protection, which will have a positive impact on their social status. To ensure such access, the state can provide subsidies for the purchase of insurance policies or benefits for companies offering special social insurance programs. Moreover, cooperation with non-profit and international organizations, such as the World Bank and the Asian Development Bank, allows attracting additional resources to finance inclusive programs, which also contributes to achieving the goals set.

2. Stimulating small- and medium-sized businesses through insurance. Small- and medium-sized businesses (SMEs) play a vital role in the economy of Uzbekistan, providing employment and making a significant contribution to the country's gross domestic product (GDP). Supporting SME entrepreneurship through business risk insurance, liability insurance, and property insurance is an important tool for increasing sector sustainability. In the context of inclusive insurance, such services should be adapted to the characteristics and needs of SMEs, especially those companies that are in the early development stages and lacking sufficient resources for full financial protection. Providing insurance solutions that are affordable in terms of cost and conditions reduces the financial burden on entrepreneurs, helps to preserve and develop their business, and reduces their vulnerability to external and internal risks, which is especially important in conditions of unstable economic factors and changing market conditions.

Table 4.3. Definitions used in model construction.

Definition	Description
R_i	Expected revenue of enterprise *i*
C_i	Total operating costs of *i* enterprise
L_i	The loss amount of enterprise *i* due to the entrepreneurial risks
$\theta_i \in [0,1]$	Degree of insurance coverage of risks (insurance efficiency)
$\alpha_i \in [0,1]$	Insurance accessibility index for enterprises
P_i	Insurance premium (depends on θ_i and α_i)
$S_i = \theta_i \bullet L_i$	Insurance indemnity in case of risk
I_i	Investments in business development
Π_i	Net profit after insurance
$U_i \in \{0,1\}$	Enterprise sustainability indicator
$\tau \in [0,1]$	Insurance protection threshold for sustainability

We have proposed a model formalizing the impact of insurance on the sustainability and development of SMEs in Uzbekistan, considering the features of inclusive insurance.

When building the model, it is assumed that $I \in \{1,2,...,N\}$ represents a small or medium enterprise operating in an unstable economic environment. The enterprise faces risks that can lead to partial or complete capital loss. Insurance is considered a tool for reducing these risks and increasing sustainability. The definitions used in building the model are provided in Table 4.3.

The net profit of the enterprise after the insurance event and receipt of insurance indemnity can be determined as

$$\Pi_i = R_i - C_i - (1 - \theta_i)\, L_i + \theta_i L_i - P_i - I_i = R_i - C_i - L_i + \theta_i L_i - P_i - I_i \Rightarrow \Pi_i = R_i - C_i - L_i\,(1 - \theta_i) - P_i - I_i.$$

We define the binary sustainability function as

$$U_i = \begin{cases} 1 & \text{if } \Pi_i > 0 \text{ and } \theta_i \cdot \alpha_i \geq \tau\, 0, \\ 0 & \text{otherwise,} \end{cases}$$

where:

- $\Pi_i \geq 0$ means financial sustainability;
- $\theta_i \cdot \alpha_i \geq \tau$ denotes the availability of sufficient insurance coverage under acceptable conditions.

Suppose that the insurance premium P_i depends linearly on the coverage level and accessibility. Then,

$$P_i = k \cdot \theta_i \cdot (1 - \alpha_i),$$

where k is the base insurance rate. The higher the accessibility *ai*, the lower the premium.

The economic contribution of all enterprises is expressed through the total net profit:

$$GDP_{MCB} = \sum_{i=1}^{N} \max(0, \Pi_i),$$

or, for sustainable business,

$$GDP^* = \sum_{i=1}^{N} U_i \Pi_i.$$

We minimize the share of unstable enterprises with the state budget constraint on insurance support:

$$\min(\theta_i, \alpha_i) \sum_{i-1}^{N} (1 - U_i),$$

with the following constraints:

- $\sum_{i-1}^{N} \sigma i \leq B,$ is a constraint on the budget for subsidizing insurance premiums, where $\sigma_i = k \cdot \theta_i \cdot (1-\alpha_i) \cdot s_i$, and $s_i \in [0,1]$ is the share of the premium subsidized by the state;
- $\vartheta_i \in [0,1]$ and $\alpha_i \in [0,1]$.

The analysis of the model allowed us to reveal that:

- an increase in θ_i reduces the damage from risks, while an increase in α_i makes insurance accessible even for poorly capitalized SMEs;
- the parameters α_i and the subsidies σ_i reflect the adaptation of insurance to the needs of start-up enterprises;
- an increase in the share of sustainable enterprises directly increases the contribution of small and private businesses to GDP.

3. Development of agricultural insurance to protect farmers.

   Agriculture plays a central role in the economy of Uzbekistan, providing employment for a large portion of the population, especially in rural areas. However, the agricultural sector is exposed to a number of risk factors, such as weather conditions, pests, and fluctuating product prices. The agricultural insurance development based on subsidized programs, under which the state supports farmers by partially covering insurance premiums, can significantly reduce financial risks of farmers and maintain their stable income. The introduction of technologies for risk assessment and loss adjustment, such as drones and satellite imagery, also makes insurance more accessible and reliable for agricultural enterprises. State programs to support farmers in this area provide insurance coverage for those who are the main source of food security in the country.
4. Introduction of digital technologies to improve access to insurance.

   Digitalization of insurance services significantly increases their accessibility for the population. In Uzbekistan, the introduction of online platforms, mobile applications, and remote claims settlement creates conditions for residents of remote areas and representatives of socially vulnerable groups to easily and promptly receive insurance services.

   Digital technologies allow not only automating processes and reducing operational costs but also providing access to insurance for those categories of the population that previously did not have the opportunity to use these services. The introduction of remote identification, digital signatures, and blockchain technology also contributes to operational transparency and customer data security, which increases the level of trust in insurance products and strengthens the relationship between insurance companies and customers.

5. Inclusive insurance programs for women and families.

   An important aspect of inclusive insurance is the development of programs focusing on supporting women and families. Such programs may include affordable health insurance for women, maternity insurance, and insurance programs for large families and single parents. Given the significant contribution of women to the economy, especially in rural areas and small businesses, such insurance programs help ensure financial security, increasing women's economic independence and strengthening families. These measures promote gender equality in financial services and stimulate economic activity, strengthening socio-economic resilience in the long term.

6. Improving the level of financial literacy and public awareness.

   One of the priorities of inclusive insurance is to educate the population about insurance products and their benefits. Insufficient financial literacy prevents the expansion of demand for insurance, especially among low-income and rural populations. Through information and educational campaigns, insurance companies and government agencies can help spread knowledge about insurance, increase trust in insurance services, and improve the overall perception of these services among the population. The development of educational initiatives, including financial courses and seminars, as well as the use of online platforms for distance learning, allows for a more effective and comprehensive approach to improving financial literacy.

7. State support and inclusive insurance stimulation.

   State support is a key factor in promoting inclusive insurance. The Government of Uzbekistan is taking steps to support the development of inclusive insurance, including programs to subsidize insurance premiums for certain population categories and introduce tax incentives for insurance companies offering socially oriented insurance products. Such measures help reduce insurance costs for vulnerable groups of the population and encourage companies to develop new inclusive products. Regulatory support, including the creation of a regulatory framework for consumer protection and the regulation of digital technologies in insurance, provides a reliable legal basis for the expansion of inclusive insurance and allows for the adaptation of insurance products to the needs of different groups of the population.

   Inclusive insurance in Uzbekistan plays an important role in the socio-economic development of the country, providing access to financial protection for all categories of the population and supporting social sustainability. Ensuring inclusive insurance requires a comprehensive approach, including the development of affordable insurance products, the introduction of digital technologies, improved financial literacy, and state support. As a result, the implementation of inclusive priorities contributes to the creation of a fair and effective insurance system that takes into account the needs of each population segment and contributes to the country's long-term sustainable economic development. A comparison of the experience of inclusive insurance in the world and in Uzbekistan is given in Table 4.4.

Inclusive insurance has already become an important tool to fight against poverty and social inequality in the world, expanding access to basic services for large sections of the population. Countries such as India, Kenya, and Brazil are actively developing microinsurance using modern technologies and regulatory mechanisms.

Table 4.4. Comparative table of inclusive insurance experience in the world and in Uzbekistan.

No.	Criteria	World Experience	Uzbekistan Experience
1.	Insurance products availability	Inclusive insurance worldwide aims to expand access for socially vulnerable groups (the poor, rural residents, women, and migrants). Affordable and flexible products such as microinsurance, health insurance, life insurance, and property insurance have been developed.	In Uzbekistan, inclusive insurance is just beginning to develop. The main focus is on the availability of products for the population living in rural areas, as well as for certain socially vulnerable groups, such as retirees, large families, and people with disabilities.
2.	Microinsurance	Microinsurance has become one of the key instruments of inclusive insurance in Asia, Africa, and Latin America. It is aimed at minimizing the cost of policies and providing simple insurance products to the poor.	Microinsurance is developing slowly in Uzbekistan. Some insurance companies have started to develop low-cost products for rural and low-income groups, but the microinsurance market as a whole has not yet been formed.
3.	Regulatory initiatives and support	In many countries, the global practice of inclusive insurance is supported at the state level. Regulators develop special programs and initiatives to increase the insurance products' availability, support legislation that promotes the microinsurance development. Some countries have developed special tax incentives and subsidies for the poor.	There is no clear state program aimed at developing inclusive insurance in Uzbekistan. However, there are some initiatives, such as the introduction of state programs to support socially vulnerable groups of the population, including in the field of healthcare. Regulatory initiatives in the field of inclusive insurance are developing slowly.
4.	Education and financial literacy	In countries with developed inclusive insurance, financial literacy programs are actively working among the population. Local and international organizations conduct training courses and information campaigns to raise awareness about insurance among low-income and vulnerable groups.	In Uzbekistan, programs to improve financial literacy among the wide population are just beginning to develop. Insurance companies conduct individual educational events, but the audience reach is limited, especially among the rural population.
5.	Role of international organizations	Many international organizations, such as the World Bank and the International Association of Insurance Supervisors (IAIS), actively support inclusive insurance, implement global standards, and conduct training projects. Partnerships between public, private, and non-profit organizations play an important role.	In Uzbekistan, international organizations actively support inclusive insurance through various projects and consultations. In particular, programs of the World Bank and other international organizations help develop approaches adapted to the country's conditions.
6.	Types of inclusive products	In international practice, inclusive insurance covers a wide range of products: micro-insurance of life, health, property, and agricultural insurance, as well as risks related to catastrophes and emergencies. Products often include simple and transparent conditions.	In Uzbekistan, basic types of inclusive insurance, such as health and life insurance for socially vulnerable groups, are offered. Products aimed at the rural population are mainly related to agricultural insurance, but their coverage is limited.
7.	Cooperation with other sectors	Countries with developed inclusive insurance actively use partnerships with various sectors: mobile operators, microfinance institutions, and NGOs. Mobile payments and partner networks help to increase the insurance availability for the poor.	In Uzbekistan, cooperation with other sectors to expand inclusive insurance is at an early stage. Some insurance companies are starting to partner with microfinance organizations and banks to expand coverage, but this is not yet a widespread practice.

In Uzbekistan, inclusive insurance is at an early development stage, with a limited range of products and limited digitalization. However, the country has significant potential for developing inclusive insurance, especially in rural areas, where a significant portion of the population does not have access to traditional insurance products.

4.3 Prospects of Green Insurance in Uzbekistan

Green insurance is a concept that aims to support sustainable development and environmental protection through insurance products and services. It includes the following aspects:

1. Development of insurance products that take into account natural risks and encourage insureds (insured persons) to use environmentally friendly technologies. For example, reducing insurance premiums for owners of electric vehicles or for companies using renewable energy sources.
2. Acceptance of obligations by insurers to reduce their carbon footprint by implementing sustainable practices into their business processes, such as reducing paper use, optimizing energy consumption, and introducing digital technologies. In addition, it helps insureds reduce their carbon footprint.
3. Ensuring sustainable insurance and promoting sustainable practices. Insurance companies provide bonuses or discounts to insureds who actively participate in environmental programs, such as recycling or using resources with minimal impact on nature.

The main characteristics of green insurance are presented in Table 4.5.

The state of green insurance practiced in the world and in Uzbekistan is presented in Table 4.6.

The prospects for green insurance in Uzbekistan look quite promising, especially given global trends toward sustainable development and environmental protection.

Key aspects contributing to the green insurance development are as follows:

1. **Government support:** The Government of Uzbekistan is actively working to improve the environmental situation in the country, creating the basis for the introduction of green insurance.
2. **Investment stimulation:** Increasing investment in environmentally friendly technologies and projects can contribute to the demand for insurance products that protect these initiatives.

Table 4.5. Key features of green insurance.

No.	Characteristic	Description
1.	Sustainable development	Supporting initiatives promoting environmental protection.
2.	Environmental risks	Assessment of risks related to climate change and natural disasters.
3.	Incentives for customers	Discounts for customers using environmentally friendly technologies.
4.	Products	Insurance for renewable energy, green vehicles and more.
5.	Social responsibility	Support for local environmental initiatives and projects.

Table 4.6. State of green insurance in world practice and Uzbekistan.

Criteria	World Practice	Uzbekistan	Analysis of Differences
1. Definition and concept	Environmental risk insurance, support for ESG principles, climate adaptation	Limited understanding, focus on renewable energy, partial implementation of green regulations	Globally – comprehensive approach; in Uzbekistan – fragmented
2. Main insurance types	Renewable energy insurance (solar and wind power plants), "green" real estate (LEED certification), eco-friendly transport (electric vehicles), agricultural insurance taking into account climate risks	Pilot projects in renewable energy sources (solar panels), lack of specialized products for "green" real estate/transport	In the world – product diversification; in Uzbekistan – narrow focus
3. Legal base	EU Solvency II Directive (ESG risks) UNEP FI, PSI principles, national climate laws (e.g. Germany, the US)	Green Economy Strategy 2030, lack of ESG regulation in insurance	In Uzbekistan – framework documents without details
4. State's role	Subsidies and tax incentives (e.g. the US – ITC for renewable energy), mandatory inclusion of ESG factors (EU)	Benefits for investors in renewable energy sources, partnership with IFIs (EBRD, World Bank)	In the world – direct regulation; in Uzbekistan – indirect support
5. Examples of products and players	Swiss Re: Climate Catastrophe Insurance, Allianz: Green Policies for Electric Cars, Lloyd's: Covering Damages from Natural Disasters	Uzbekinvest JSC: insurance of solar power plants, Uzagrosugurta JSC: individual environmental risks	In Uzbekistan – rare cases, absence of branded products
6. Market volume	EU: €20+ billion (2023), US: US$15 billion. (renewable energy sector)	Less than US$1 million. (estimate, 2023)	Uzbekistan's share is less than 0.1% of the global market
7. Challenges	High volatility of climate risks, need for long-term data	Underwriting weaknesses, low demand from businesses, lack of actuarial models for local risks	The key issue in Uzbekistan is infrastructure and educational gaps
8. Trends	Growth of catastrophe insurance (floods, droughts), development of index insurance, blockchain integration for transparency	Gradual implementation of international standards, potential for drought-sensitive agricultural insurance	Uzbekistan can use global experience, bypassing the trial-and-error stages

3. **Raising awareness:** With the growing interest in environmental issues among the population and businesses, the need to protect against environmental risks through insurance is also on the rise.
4. **Cooperation with international organizations:** Uzbekistan can attract international funds and organizations to finance and develop green insurance products.
5. **Development of new products:** Insurance companies can develop special products covering risks related to climate change, pollution, and other environmental issues.
6. **Sustainable agriculture:** Agricultural risk insurance with an emphasis on sustainable practices can become an important part of green insurance.
7. **Climate change:** The increasing frequency and severity of climate events create a need for insurance against the risks related to them.

In detail, the state's support in the green insurance field in Uzbekistan can be seen in several key initiatives and programs:

1. **National Environmental Strategy:** Uzbekistan has developed a sustainable development strategy that emphasizes environmental protection. This strategy may define measures to introduce green insurance as a tool for protecting environmental projects.
2. **Green economy legislation:** Adoption of laws regulating environmental activities and green investments creates a legal basis for the development of insurance products aimed at protecting the environment.
3. **Programs to support environmentally friendly technologies:** Uzbekistan is implementing programs aimed at supporting the introduction of environmentally friendly technologies in agriculture and industry. Insurance companies can offer products that cover the risks of these initiatives.
4. **State grants and subsidies:** Allocation of budget funds for environmental projects may increase demand for insurance on these projects, protecting investors from environmental risks.
5. **Educational initiatives:** Awareness-raising programs among the public and businesses about the importance of ecology and environmental risks can create a basis for popularizing green insurance.
6. **Cooperation with international partners:** Uzbekistan cooperates with international environmental organizations, which can help in developing standards for green insurance and attracting external financing.

Growth of investment in clean technologies and projects can significantly increase demand for insurance products that protect these initiatives. Key areas for stimulating investment in clean technologies and projects include:

- providing financial support for start-ups and clean technology companies, as well as grants for research and development in sustainable technologies;
- introduction of tax breaks for companies investing in environmentally friendly projects and exemption from income tax for enterprises implementing green technologies;
- establishment of investment funds specializing in environmentally friendly projects that will attract private investment and support for international financing and cooperation;
- conducting seminars and trainings for investors, informing about opportunities in the field of green technologies, and forming a platform for uniting investors and environmentally friendly projects.

Table 4.7. Cooperation with international organizations and funds.

Organization/Foundation	Role and Contribution
World Bank	Financing projects aimed at sustainable development
Global Environment Facility	Supporting initiatives to combat climate change
United Nations Environment Programme	Consulting and expertise in the field of ecology
European Union	Provision of grants and technical assistance

Stimulating investment in green technologies and projects not only helps protect the environment but also creates new opportunities for insurance companies. Increasing the number of projects and demand for insurance products will ensure sustainable development for both businesses and the ecosystem as a whole.

Raising awareness of green insurance plays a key role in shaping a sustainable future. As interest in ecology increases, the need to protect against environmental risks grows, which in turn creates new opportunities for both businesses and insurance companies. Raising awareness of green insurance can be achieved in the following ways:

- conducting informational seminars and webinars aimed at explaining the benefits of green insurance and preparing educational materials, including brochures, articles, and videos, accessible to a wide audience;
- organizing meetings, round tables, and conferences, where business representatives can discuss the importance of protection against the consequences of environmental risks;
- developing online resources and applications to help users better understand how green insurance can protect their projects and disseminating information through social networks to reach a wide audience.

Cooperation with international funds and organizations can significantly accelerate the development of green insurance in Uzbekistan. This will not only help support environmentally friendly initiatives but also create a financial safety net for businesses and the population facing the effects of climate change. Investments and expertise from international partners can help create a more sustainable and adaptive insurance system that will take into account environmental risks and support sustainable development. Examples of cooperation with international organizations and funds are given in Table 4.7.

One of the key aspects that contributes to green insurance development is the development and implementation of new insurance products. Insurers can develop specialized products that cover risks related to climate change, pollution, and other environmental issues.

Potential insurance products may include:

- climate risk insurance (protection against losses, caused by extreme weather events such as floods, droughts, and hurricanes);
- environmental projects insurance (support for initiatives on renewable energy sources and sustainable development);
- environmental liability insurance (protection of insureds against financial consequences related to environmental pollution);
- insurance of agricultural risks (products covering risks related to climate change for agricultural producers).

Development of such products will allow insurers not only to expand their business but also to actively contribute to the sustainable development of society and environmental protection.

Green insurance in agriculture can protect farmers from losses; it also contributes to the sustainable development of the agricultural sector, ensuring food security and supporting ecosystems in the following ways:

- insurance protection against the consequences of climate change risks, such as droughts, floods, heavy rains, and dry winds;
- stimulating the use of sustainable agricultural production practices by agricultural producers;
- support for innovation through participation in financing and subsidizing new agricultural technologies (drip irrigation, technologies that increase fertility and reduce soil erosion, etc.).

The development of effective insurance products focused on risks related to climate change is becoming an important step toward sustainable development and protection against potential losses. The main characteristics of green insurance products from leading foreign insurers are provided in Table 4.8.

Table 4.8. Key characteristics of green insurance products by leading foreign insurance companies.

Insurance Company	Products and Services	Key Characteristics	Geographical Coverage	Sustainable Development Initiatives
Allianz	Environmental risk insurance, green policies for businesses and individuals, support for sustainable projects	Developed green products for renewable energy and sustainable technology companies	The European Union, the US, Asia	Incorporating environmental factors into policies, participating in the Principles of Sustainable Insurance (PSI) initiative, supporting the transition to a low-carbon economy, enhancing climate resilience through products
AXA	Natural disaster and climate protection insurance, policies for clean energy projects	Offers tailored solutions for environmental risk protection and green energy investments	Worldwide	Supporting the PSI initiative, financing and insuring environmentally sustainable projects, reducing carbon risks, creating green investment products
Zurich	Climate change insurance, green products for businesses	Developed solutions for businesses, taking into account environmental risks and sustainable technologies	Europe, North America, Asia	Investments in green projects, attention to climate risks in insurance, development of products for the protection of ecosystems and renewable energy sources, participation in sustainable business initiatives

(*Continued*)

Table 4.8. (*Continued*)

Insurance Company	Products and Services	Key Characteristics	Geographical Coverage	Sustainable Development Initiatives
Swiss Re	Climate risk insurance, environmental risk analysis for businesses and private clients	Application of innovative technologies for climate risk analysis, participation in global sustainable development initiatives	Worldwide	Active participation in climate risk research, support for green technologies, assistance in developing solutions to protect against natural disasters, creating a climate for sustainable development through insurance
Munich Re	Carbon risk insurance, policies for green projects, and renewable energy sources	Developing products that support carbon reduction initiatives, protecting green businesses	Europe, Asia, the US	Offering innovative solutions for carbon risk management, participating in global sustainable development initiatives, developing products to protect ecosystems and improve environmental sustainability.
Generali	Environmental risk insurance, support for green projects and businesses, green investment solutions	Insurance for renewable energy, sustainable agriculture, and ecotourism projects	Europe, Asia, Latin America	Developing solutions to support sustainable business, reducing risks to ecosystems and natural resources, implementing green insurance standards, participating in international initiatives
MetLife	Natural disaster protection products, sustainable insurance for corporate clients	Offers insurance for companies working with green technologies and for projects that minimize their carbon footprint	The US, Asia, Latin America	Focus on supporting sustainable initiatives for businesses and private clients, participation in the development of environmentally friendly solutions and green technologies
Aviva	Natural disaster insurance, ecosystem protection, green insurance for corporate clients	Incorporating environmental risks into insurance products for companies operating in environmentally friendly sectors	The UK, Europe, Asia	Sustainability programs, support for low carbon solutions, participation in the PSI initiative and development of flexible solutions to protect against environmental risks

Table 4.8. (*Continued*)

Insurance Company	Products and Services	Key Characteristics	Geographical Coverage	Sustainable Development Initiatives
Chubb	Environmental risk insurance, protection against environmental disasters and man-made accidents	Offers business insurance, including policies to protect against pollution and natural disasters	The US, Europe, Asia	Support for green initiatives, participation in sustainable insurance programs, financing projects aimed at reducing environmental impact
Lloyd's of London	Specialized policies to protect against climate and environmental risks, development of new insurance solutions	Provides a platform for the development of unique insurance products, including environmental risks	Worldwide	Actively develops insurance for climate risks and risks related to natural disasters, cooperates with various countries to provide effective solutions for green insurance
State Farm	Natural catastrophe insurance, sustainable insurance for individuals and businesses	Developing products to protect against environmental risks, including earthquakes, floods, and fires	The US	Climate risk protection programs, support for sustainable development initiatives, and eco-consciousness in insurance products
Suncorp	Insurance for clients working in the field of sustainable agriculture and renewable energy	Development of insurance products for farmers and businesses using sustainable agricultural practices	Australia, New Zealand, Asia	Specializing in green insurance for agriculture and clean technologies, participating in the initiative for sustainable development and reducing environmental impact
Prudential	Insurance for renewable energy and green building projects	Insurance for residential and commercial properties with sustainability and energy efficiency	The UK, the US, Asia	Developing products to support green building initiatives, reducing carbon risks in the corporate sector, and actively participating in international sustainable development programs
Farmers Insurance	Natural disaster insurance, policies for the protection of natural resources and ecosystems	Products for private and corporate clients that support sustainable land and natural resource management	The US, Canada	Developing programs to protect ecosystems, participating in initiatives to conserve natural resources, collaborating with clients to develop environmentally friendly solutions

Green insurance and ESG transformation are becoming the main directions in the development of modern insurance businesses. These concepts not only contribute to the sustainability of companies but also help them adapt to challenges related to climate change and social responsibility.

Green insurance and ESG transformation are permanently linked, as both approaches aim to build a sustainable future. Green insurance supports ESG principles, helping insurance companies reduce their environmental impact and improve their social responsibility.

Green insurance and ESG transformation are important strategic directions for the insurance business, contributing to the creation of a sustainable future. These approaches help insurers adapt to modern challenges, improving their reputation and ensuring long-term profitability. Integrating ESG aspects into the business models of insurance companies not only meets current requirements but also creates new opportunities for growth and development in a changing world.

Green insurance, which includes insurance products aimed at supporting sustainable development and minimizing environmental impact, is an important component of modern insurance practices. While this area is actively developing worldwide, green insurance is still at the initial stage of its formation in Uzbekistan. It is important to analyze the current status and prospects for green insurance development in Uzbekistan, taking into account global experience and local realities (Table 4.9).

Table 4.9. Prospects for the green insurance development in Uzbekistan.

No.	Key Field	Current Status in Uzbekistan	Initiatives and Development Prospects
1.	Regulatory base	Uzbekistan currently lacks specific legislation regulating green insurance. Instead, more general environmental regulations are being developed to address environmental protection and sustainable development.	It is expected that laws will be adopted to stimulate the green insurance development, including the creation of mechanisms to support climate adaptation and protection against environmental risks.
2.	Environmental Insurance	At present, there are no products in the country that focus on insuring environmental risks such as water, soil, and air pollution. Insurance companies mainly offer traditional products that do not take environmental threats into account.	It is expected that new products will be introduced to insure risks related to environmental disasters, such as pollution of natural resources, which will become a significant part of green insurance.
3.	Insurance of energy efficient objects	In Uzbekistan, there are no insurance products aimed at insuring objects, taking into account energy efficiency or the use of environmentally friendly technologies in construction and real estate.	The development of products focused on green construction and insurance of facilities certified according to such international environmental standards as LEED or BREEAM is expected.
4.	Agricultural risk insurance in the context of sustainability	Agricultural risk insurance is currently actively developing in Uzbekistan, but it does not include aspects related to resilience to climate change, such as drought or extreme weather conditions.	In the future, it is expected that there will be development of products that take into account climate change and the risks related to its impact on agriculture, which will increase the resilience of the rural sector to extreme weather events.

Table 4.9. (*Continued*)

No.	Key Field	Current Status in Uzbekistan	Initiatives and Development Prospects
5.	Innovations and new products	In Uzbekistan, the green insurance sector lacks innovative products aimed at stimulating environmentally responsible behavior. For example, there are no discounts for using energy-efficient technologies or environmentally friendly vehicles.	New products are expected to be developed, such as discounts on policies for owners of electric vehicles or for companies that use environmentally friendly technologies in their operations.
6.	Education and raising awareness	In Uzbekistan, awareness of green insurance is inadequate. To date, there are no large-scale educational campaigns to raise awareness of the population and businesses about green insurance products.	Educational programs and information campaigns are expected to raise awareness of the importance of green insurance, as well as to involve insurance companies in developing environmentally responsible products.
7.	International cooperation	At present, international cooperation in the field of green insurance is limited in Uzbekistan. However, there are programs of international financial institutions aimed at improving the environmental situation.	Developing cooperation with such international organizations as the World Bank and the United Nations Environment Programme (UNEP) can play a key role in introducing green insurance products and technologies in Uzbekistan.
8.	Climate and environmental legislation	Uzbekistan is already implementing a number of environmental initiatives aimed at reducing carbon emissions and protecting natural resources. However, legislation regulating environmental insurance has not yet been formed.	In the long term, legislation should include measures to incentivize green insurance, including taxes and subsidies for companies using sustainable environmental practices.
9.	Development prospects	Green insurance in Uzbekistan is at the initial stage. Insurance products focused on sustainable development and environmental risks are not developed.	In the future, green insurance could become an important part of the market if regulations are put in place and awareness-raising activities are carried out among consumers and businesses.

Green insurance in Uzbekistan is at an early development stage, and its implementation will require the formation of an appropriate legislative framework, educational programs, and increased awareness among the population and business community. At the same time, given global trends and the need to adapt to the challenges of climate change, Uzbekistan has significant prospects for integrating environmentally sustainable practices into the insurance sector.

Green insurance is an important and developing area that plays a key role in adapting the economy and society to environmental challenges, given the growing risks related to climate change and environmental disasters. In the Uzbek context, as a country striving for sustainable economic development and overcoming environmental problems, the effective implementation of green insurance can become a significant tool in carrying out state environmental policy and supporting the sustainability of natural and economic systems. Let us consider the main areas of green insurance research and application, paying special attention to the specifics of Uzbekistan.

Research in the green insurance field highlights the importance of involving insurance companies in the management of environmental risks such as climate change, natural disasters, pollution, and biodiversity loss. In Uzbekistan, where climate change is already taking place in the form of droughts, falling water levels, and more frequent extreme weather events, insurance companies can play an important role in forming effective risk management mechanisms. The use of innovative insurance products that take into account these environmental factors will help minimize damage to individual households, large enterprises, and government agencies. An important aspect is the need to develop environmental risk assessment models that can take into account the specific climatic and natural conditions of Uzbekistan.

For the full development of green insurance in Uzbekistan, it is necessary to develop and implement a clear normative and regulatory framework meeting international standards and principles of sustainable development. An important step in this direction are initiatives such as the Principles of Sustainable Insurance (PSI), which involve the integration of environmental risks and social factors into insurance products and services. In Uzbekistan, the development of a regulatory system supporting sustainable insurance initiatives will be key to the successful implementation of green insurance products and will help eliminate legal barriers to their development. In addition, it is necessary to pay attention to synchronization with such international initiatives as the United Nations Environment Programme, and the integration of these principles into national legislation.

Green insurance should not only minimize environmental risks but also promote environmental awareness among consumers. This requires the development of innovative insurance products that help reduce carbon emissions and support green technologies. For Uzbekistan, this is especially relevant in the context of active work to introduce renewable energy sources, energy efficiency, and sustainable agriculture. Insurance companies can offer products that will cover the risks related to the use of environmentally friendly technologies and also stimulate more sustainable behavior among consumers. For example, insurance for businesses implementing energy-efficient technologies or for farmers using sustainable agricultural methods can be an important step toward the sustainable development of the country's economy.

One of the significant aspects of green insurance is its impact on corporate social responsibility (CSR). In Uzbekistan, where many companies are beginning to realize their role in solving environmental issues, green insurance can become an important part of corporate strategy. Insurance focused on reducing environmental risks can encourage businesses to implement more sustainable practices in their operations. The use of such products will help popularize eco-conscious business decisions and help companies meet global sustainability standards.

The prospects for the green insurance development in Uzbekistan are related to several key areas. Firstly, this involves the deeper integration of environmental risks into financial regulation and the insurance market, which will increase financial stability and reduce risks for the economy. Secondly, this is the new insurance product development aimed at protecting against environmental threats, as well as ensuring sustainable agriculture, urban, and industrial development. Thirdly, an important element is the strengthening of international cooperation to harmonize standards, exchange experience, and implement best practices in the green insurance field.

Green insurance in Uzbekistan is an important area for the development of a sustainable economy focused on solving environmental issues and overcoming the challenges related to climate change. The creation and implementation of an effective regulatory framework, the development of innovative insurance products, and raising awareness among consumers are the most important aspects that will allow this area to develop. In the future, green insurance can play a key role in ensuring the sustainability of economic and natural systems in Uzbekistan, supporting sustainable development and achieving the goals of national environmental policy.

The green insurance prospects in the country are directly related to the need to increase the role of environmental standards in construction, agriculture, and other sectors of the economy. In the future, this area may become not only an important part of the protection system against environmental risks but also a way to stimulate economic activity within the framework of sustainable development.

4.4 Conclusions

1. Integration of digital technologies with ESG principles is becoming a key driver of modernization in the insurance sector of Uzbekistan, ensuring the growth of customer service, efficiency, and risk management. Automation of processes (online sales, underwriting, and claims settlement) significantly reduces costs: In Uzbekinvest, for example, policy processing has been reduced from 8 to 0.5 minutes. The use of AI, RPA, telematics, and biometrics increases accuracy and reduces the fraud level.

   Despite the technological lag behind developed markets, Uzbekistan has demonstrated progress in developing digital infrastructure (data warehouse and scoring). The main barriers – regulatory gaps and qualified personnel shortage – require institutional reforms and investments in digital literacy. The potential of digitalization, confirmed by modeling, can be realized with active government support, transforming the insurance sector into an instrument of sustainable growth and ESG integration.
2. Inclusive insurance based on ESG principles forms a new insurance market model focused on social accessibility and sustainability. It includes customer centricity, digital solutions (mobile platforms and e-ID), educational initiatives, and support for vulnerable groups (rural population, small businesses, and low-income families). These elements ensure expanded coverage and help reduce social inequality.

   In Uzbekistan, there is a certain growth in microinsurance and agricultural insurance policies with state support, but digitalization and the regulatory framework remain at an early stage. To scale the model, tax incentives, partnerships with IFIs, the introduction of technologies (AI and blockchain), and localization of international practices are necessary. Inclusive insurance with a systematic approach can become a tool for economic sustainability and social integration.
3. "Green" insurance, as an element of ESG transformation, is becoming a promising vector for modernizing the insurance market of Uzbekistan. Its triple impact – environmental (climate risk insurance and support for renewable energy sources), economic (tariff incentives for "green" technologies), and social (raising environmental awareness) – creates a new institutional logic. However, the sector is at an early stage: There is no specialized regulation, the product line is limited, and the incentive system is underdeveloped.

A systematic approach is necessary for development: international standards adaptation (PSI), introduction of tax incentives, launch of climate-oriented products (insurance for agriculture, renewable energy sources, and "green" construction), formation of a pool of environmental risks, and partnerships with global institutions. Pilot projects, industry standards, and PPPs can provide synergy with national environmental programs. The potential of green insurance in Uzbekistan is due to the need to adapt to climate challenges and the pursuit of sustainable economic growth.

Chapter 5

Issues and Prospects of ESG Insurance Transformation in Uzbekistan

5.1 Current State of the Insurance Business and the Practice of Implementing ESG Standards in the Insurance Market of Uzbekistan

The insurance business in Uzbekistan has demonstrated steady growth in recent years due to a number of factors, such as economic reforms aimed at creating a favorable business environment, a gradual increase in the level of financial literacy of the population, and growing interest in insurance products from businesses and the population. The introduction of new market mechanisms, support for entrepreneurship, and an improved investment climate stimulate the insurance sector's development, contributing to the growth of insurance premiums, insurance product diversification, and an increase in the number of market participants. As a result, Uzbekistan is gradually approaching international standards of insurance activities, integrating modern risk management practices and developing more comprehensive insurance solutions that meet customer requirements.

Due to the reforms carried out as a result of the initiative of President Sh. M. Mirziyoyev, the domestic insurance market development in recent years has been characterized by high dynamics (Fig. 5.1).

The insurance market of Uzbekistan is in the process of active transformation facilitated by state reforms, digitalization, and growing demand for insurance services. The dynamics of key financial indicators for 2020–2024 are presented in Table 5.1.

As is known, the main macroeconomic indicators characterizing the insurance market are the following:

- gross premium written (GPW);
- share of GPW in gross domestic product (insurance penetration rate);
- insurance density (the amount of the insurance premium, per capita);
- loss ratio (ratio of total insurance indemnities to GPW).

Analysis of the GPW dynamics for 1997–2020, presented in Fig. 5.2, shows that in 2017–2023, the GPW increased by more than 1827 times. Some decrease in the GPW dynamics in 2020 compared to 2019 is explained by the consequences of the COVID-19 pandemic.

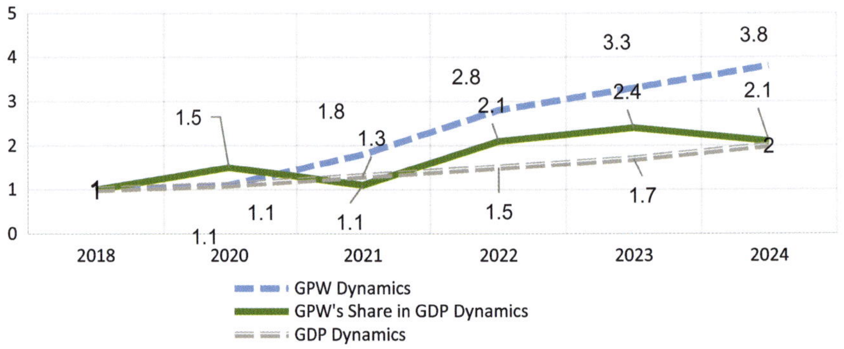

Fig. 5.1. Dynamics of GDP, GPW, and GPW share in GDP (the 2018 level is assumed to be equal to one) for 2018–2024 years period.

Source: Developed by the author based on data from the website of the National Agency of Perspective Projects of the Republic of Uzbekistan. https://napp.uz/en/pages/statistics-and-analysis-for-im.

Table 5.1. Financial indicators of the insurance market of Uzbekistan (billion Soums).

Indicator	2020	2021	2022	2023	2024
Insurance Premiums Collected	2313.9	2213.7	6231.7	8059.7	9770.1
Non-life Insurance Premiums	1727.5	1879.3	4707	7737.2	9483.7
Compulsory Insurance	298.1	338.0	491.3	632.4	664.7
Voluntary Insurance	1429.4	1541.3	4215.7	7104.8	8819.0
Life Insurance Premiums	586.4	334.4	1524.7	322.5	286.4
Compulsory Insurance	15.2	22.9	26.8	35.6	48.2
Voluntary Insurance	571.2	311.5	1497.9	286.9	238.2
Insurance Indemnities (total)	831.5	737.6	2596.9	2022.1	2204.5
Non-life Insurance Indemnities	284.1	419.6	1098.8	1568.5	2073.1
Compulsory Insurance	90.2	128.0	232.8	236.7	358.6
Voluntary Insurance	193.9	291.6	866.0	1331.8	1714.5
Life Insurance Indemnities	529.4	318.0	1498.1	453.6	131.4
Compulsory Insurance	4.3	5.7	9.3	12.7	14.7
Voluntary Insurance	525.1	312.3	1488.8	440.9	116.7

Source: Developed by the author based on data from the website of the National Agency of Perspective Projects of the Republic of Uzbekistan. https://napp.uz/en/pages/statistics-and-analysis-for-im.

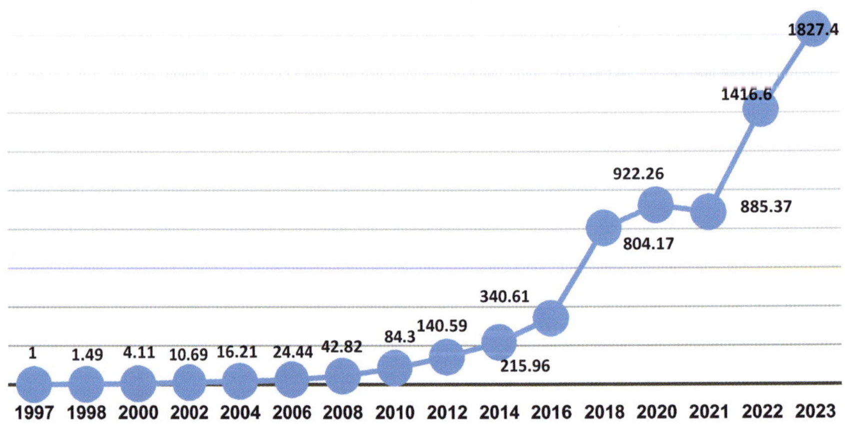

Fig. 5.2. Dynamics of GPW for the period 1997–2023 (1997 level is assumed to be equal to one).

Source: Developed by the author based on data from www.mf.uz website.

The most significant macroeconomic indicator of the importance of insurance is the ratio of gross premiums written to the gross domestic product (insurance penetration rate); in Uzbekistan, the value of this indicator in recent years has been in the range of 0.35–0.8% (Fig. 5.3).

The importance of insurance is determined by the insurance density; in Uzbekistan, according to the results of 2023, the volume of insurance premium per capita amounted to just over 18$US (Fig. 5.4).

A specific feature of insurance development in Uzbekistan in recent years remains the fact that the gross premium written for compulsory insurance types, despite the entry into force of new compulsory insurance types, did not exceed a third of the total gross premium written, and the growth of the gross premium written in the market was ensured by increases in rates for imputed and voluntary insurance types (Fig. 5.5).

The level of rates for insurance services in recent years has been determined exclusively by market conditions (Fig. 5.6). At the same time, the intention of individual new insurers to quickly increase their market share through dumping, in the absence of strict requirements regarding the ratio of insurance liabilities to insurance reserves, often leads to the settlement of insurance services tariffs at an insufficiently justified low level.

Analysis of the insurance premium loss ratio (the ratio of insurance indemnities to insurance premiums) in the non-life insurance industry for 2015–2023 reveals the extremely uneven dynamics of this indicator (Fig. 5.7). The value of this indicator for

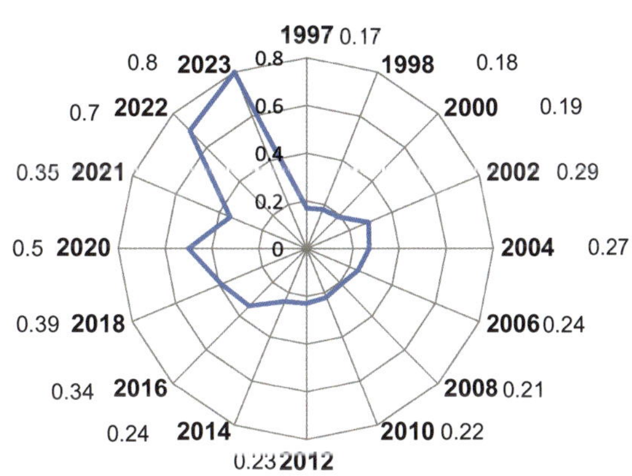

Fig. 5.3. Share of GPW in GDP (%).

Source: Developed by the author based on data from the www.mf.uz website.

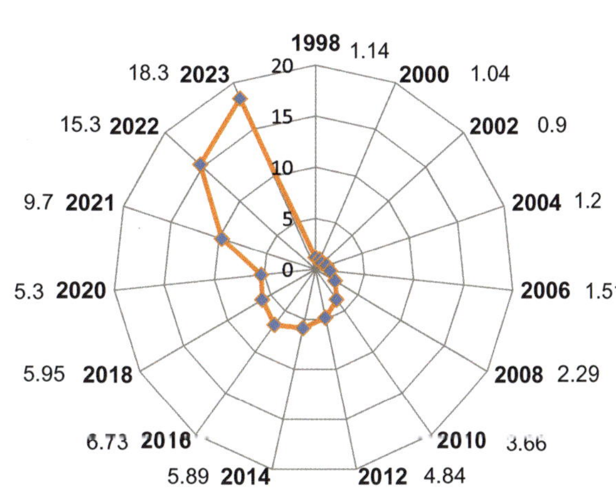

Fig. 5.4. Insurance density in Uzbekistan (in US dollars by the official exchange rate).

Source: Developed by the author based on data from the www.mf.uz website.

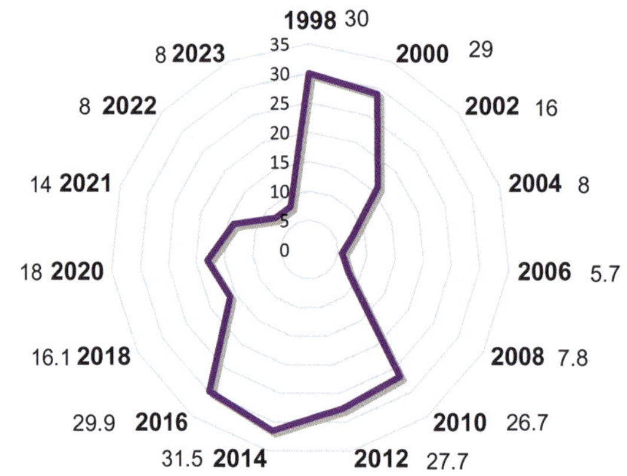

Fig. 5.5. Share of compulsory insurance types in the gross premiums written (%).
Source: Developed by the author based on data from the www.mf.uz website.

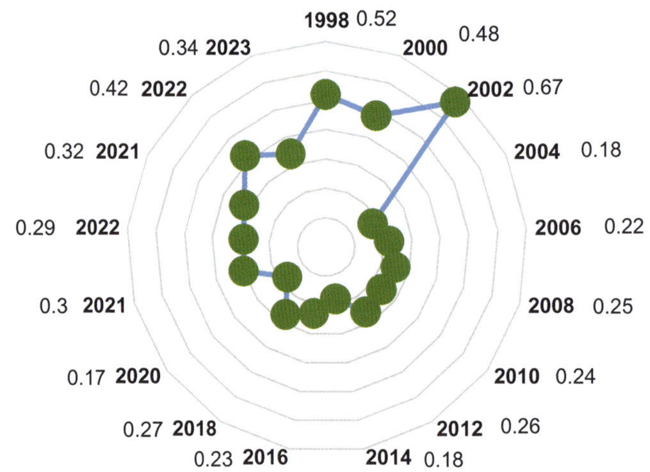

Fig. 5.6. Gross premiums written ratio to total insurance liability (average market rate) for 1998–2022 (%).
Source: Developed by the author based on data from the www.mf.uz website.

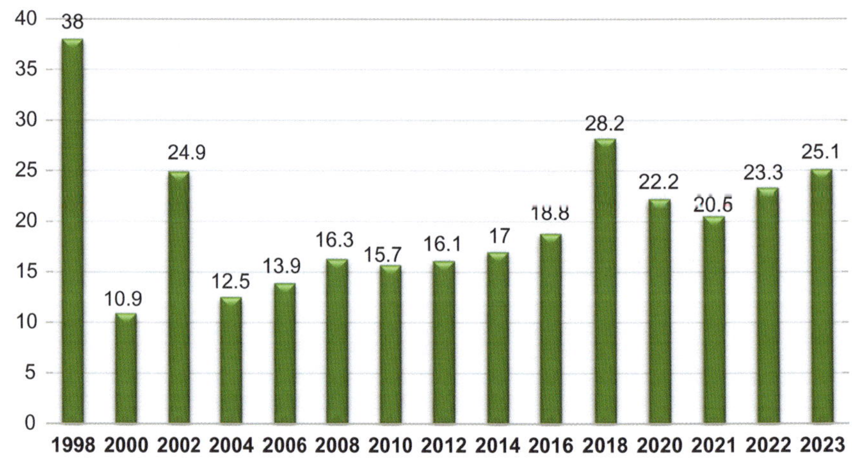

Fig. 5.7. Dynamics of the insurance premium loss ratio in the non-life insurance industry.
Source: Developed by the author based on data from the www.mf.uz website.

Table 5.2. Insurance market structure in the republic of Uzbekistan in 2016–2024.

Years	Number of Insurance Companies	Including Life Insurance	Total Share Capital of Insurance Companies (in USD million.)	Number of Insurance Brokers	Number of Certified Actuaries	Number of Insurance Agents	Number of Insurance Surveyors and Adjusters	Number of Assistance Services
2016	29	3	137.1	3	4	5,800	12	6
2018	30	6	125.1	4	4	8,700	18	6
2020	40	8	137.4	5	5	8,870	18	6
2021	42	8	146.7	5	5	9,581	18	6
2022	41	8	167.8	5	5	9,155	18	6
2023	38	7	187.0	8	5	4,736	18	6
2024	33	5	229.0	11	5	4,804	18	6

Source: Developed by the author based on data from the website of the National Agency of Perspective Projects of the Republic of Uzbekistan. https://napp.uz/en/pages/statistics-and-analysis-for-im.

domestic insurance companies in recent years has been in the range of 18.8–28.2% (Fig. 5.7), given that the loss ratio of Gosstrakh Uzbekistan for 1991–1996 was at the level of 45–60%.

The insurance market structure in 2018–2024 is represented in Table 5.2. In the Uzbek insurance market, in the first half of 2024, 35 insurers operated, 5 of which were in the life insurance industry. Despite a 14.6% drop in the number of insurance companies, their total authorized capital increased by 10.5%, reaching 2.3 trillion Soums, and the total investment volume increased by 17.8% to 6.1 trillion Soums, which indicates the stability and potential of the sector. Total insurance premiums increased by 13%, amounting to 4.2 trillion Soums, indicating a growing interest of insureds in insurance services. At the same time, insurance indemnity payments increased by 26.4%, reaching 1.1 trillion Soums, which may indicate a larger number of insured risks and increased liability of insurers.

The situation in the insurance market from a monopolization standpoint is considered competitive when the major share of total insurance premium is generated by 10 or more competitors. At the same time, the largest share held by any one of them should not exceed 31% of the total insurance premium volume; for two entities, the limit is 44%; for three, it is 54%; and for four, it is 64%[1] – the state of the insurance market of Uzbekistan meets these requirements (Table 5.3).

The share of insurance premiums in GDP at 0.8% underlines the importance of insurance in the economy, opening up new opportunities for development and improving the financial literacy of the population. Such growth can further strengthen confidence in insurance products and expand their availability.

In general, the insurance market of the republic is developing at a stable and sustainable pace, as shown in Fig. 5.8. An increase in the volume of insurance premiums, the development of new types of insurance, foreign investment attraction, an increase in

[1]R. Kayumov: "Indicators for Assessing the Monopolization Level of Financial Markets and the Possibility of Their Use in Uzbekistan" https://training-center.uz/publ-80.

Table 5.3. Leading companies by market share in the non-life insurance industry in 2017–2024.

	Market Share, %							
Company	**2017**	**2018**	**2019**	**2020**	**2021**	**2022**	**2023**	**2024**
1. Apex Insurance JSC	–	–	2,3	6,4	8,1	16,4	26,0	29,1
2. Uzbekinvest JSC	14,1	14,1	16,5	14,0	13,4	16,0	15,9	13,4
3. Kafolat JSC	8,7	8,7	8,7	8,0	7,7	7,2	9,1	7,8
4. Gross Insurance JSC	8,8	8,8	12,8	13,4	8,6	6,1	5,8	6,6
5. My Insurance JSC	–	–	2,3	5,4	8,1	5,5	4,4	4,5
6. Uzagrosugurta JSC	14,5	14,4	14,6	9,5	6,2	7,8	5,1	4,4
7. Kapital sug'urta JSC	2,7	3,0	2,7	2,6	4,4	3,6	3,9	3,9
8. Kafil sug'urta JSC	1,4	1,3	2,3	2,7	4,2	3,0	5,1	3,0
9. Alfa Invest Sug'urta Kompaniyasi JSC	5,0	5,0	5,5	5,2	5,2	6,5	3,0	2,8
10. Alskom JSC	4,2	4,2	2,8	2,3	1,7	2,0	1,9	2,1

Source: Developed by the author based on data from the website of the National Agency of Perspective Projects of the Republic of Uzbekistan. https://napp.uz/en/pages/statistics-and-analysis-for-im.

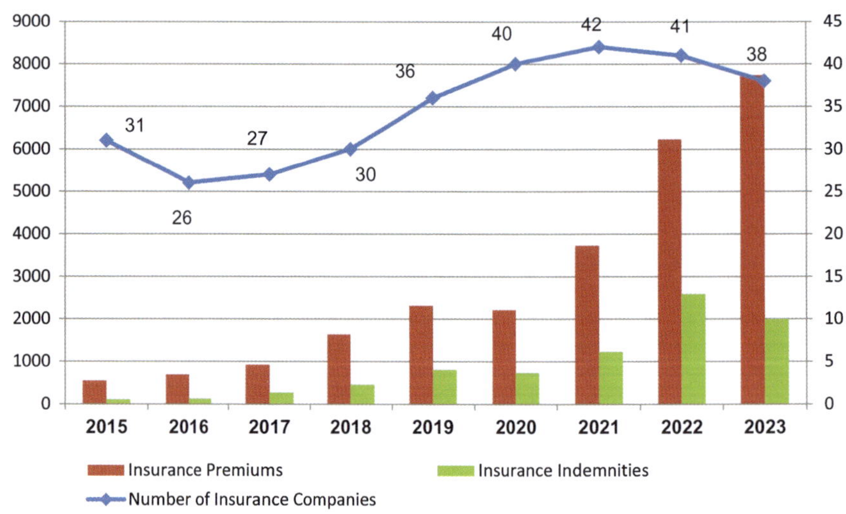

Fig. 5.8. Key indicators of the insurance market of Uzbekistan for 2015–2023.

financial literacy among the population, and the active introduction of digital technologies create a favorable basis for further growth and modernization of the insurance market.

Positive trends observed in the insurance market of Uzbekistan indicate significant changes that contribute to the strengthening of this sector and its integration into the international community (Fig. 5.9). However, to achieve long-term sustainability, it is necessary to continue working on improving legislation and stimulating demand for insurance products.

To forecast the prospects for the insurance market development in Uzbekistan, we used econometric modeling with an extended regression model that takes into account GDP, income per capita, and the level of insurance culture (financial literacy).

The volume of insurance premiums collected (in billion Soums) is considered a dependent variable. The following were selected as independent variables:

GDP – gross domestic product;

I – income per capita;

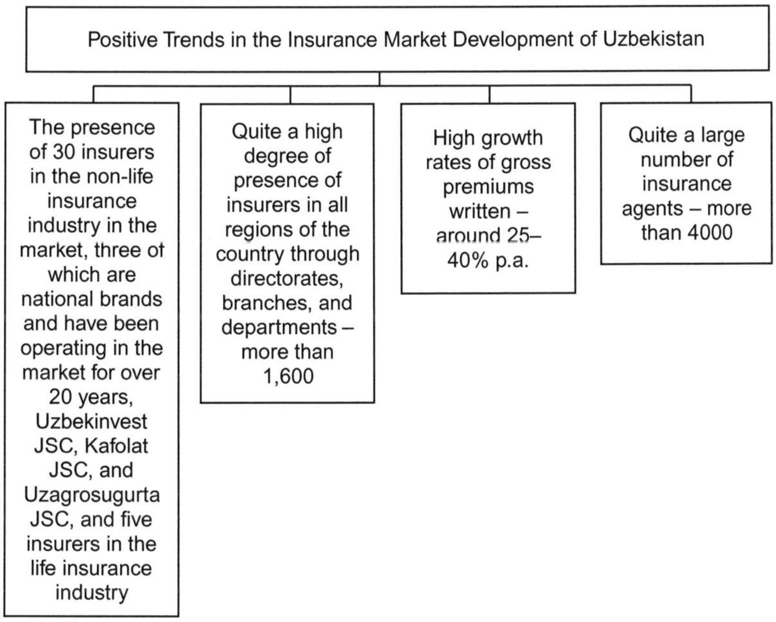

Fig. 5.9. Positive trends in the insurance market development.

Table 5.4. Grounds for the selection of factors.

No.	Factor	Reason
1.	GDP	Economic activity indicator. Insurance grows with growth of business and income.
2.	Income per capita	Shows the population solvency.
3.	Insurance culture, financial literacy level	One of the keys to making an informed insurance choice.
4.	Inflation	Affects real income and insurance activity.
5.	Interest rates	Determine the investment attractiveness of insurance company's assets.

FLI – financial literacy index (expert assessment on a scale of 0–100 points);
If – inflation rate;
IR – interest rate on deposits.

The rationale behind choosing the above factors is provided in Table 5.4.
We used a linear multiple regression model of the following type:

$$V_t = \beta_0 + \beta_1 \cdot GDP_t + \beta_2 \cdot I_t + \beta_3 \cdot FLI_t + \beta_4 \cdot If_t + \beta_5 \cdot IR_t + \epsilon_t,$$

where:
V_t – the insurance premiums volume in year t;
β_0 – a constant (the base value of insurance premiums under the condition of zero values for all factors);
GDP_t – gross domestic product in year t;
$\beta_1 \cdot$ – a coefficient taking into account the change in the insurance premiums volume under GDP increase;
I_t – income per capita in year t;

β_2· – a coefficient taking into account the change in the insurance premiums volume with income per capita increase;

FLI_t – the index of insurance culture and financial literacy in year t (a composite indicator reflecting the knowledge level, attitudes, and behavior of people in the field of personal finance and insurance);

β_3 – a coefficient taking into account the level of insurance culture and financial literacy;

If_t – inflation in year t;

β_4 – a coefficient taking into account the inflation rate;

IR_t – the interest rate on deposits in year t;

β_5 – a coefficient taking into account the change in the interest rate on deposits;

ϵ_t – model error taking into account the influence of factors not included in the model.

The initial data for 2018–2024 used in the regression model are presented in Table 5.5.

The values of the regression model coefficients obtained through estimation using the ordinary least squares (OLS) method are presented in Table 5.6.

The determination coefficient (R^2) was equal to 0.963, indicating high model accuracy. Analysis of the regression model showed that the key factors of insurance market growth are:

- growth of gross domestic product (GDP);
- improvement of the living standard (income per capita);
- growth of insurance culture (financial literacy).

The active introduction of digital technologies in insurance is another important trend that helps not only to simplify access to insurance services but also to increase their availability. In Uzbekistan, insurance companies are beginning to actively use mobile applications, online platforms, and digital sales channels, which significantly improves customer experience and contributes to the growth of the number of users of insurance services. The assessment of the achieved digitalization level of the main types of insurance activities in Uzbekistan is presented in Fig. 5.10. It is expected that digitalization will continue to develop over the coming years, making insurance a more convenient and faster process for the end consumer.

Table 5.5. Initial data for the regression model.

Year	GDP (trillion Soums)	*I* (million Soums)	*FLI**	*If* (%)	*IR* (%)	Insurance Premiums (trillion Soums)
2018	407.5	9,1	15	14.3	15.0	
2019	511.8	10,9	18	15.2	14.5	2,13
2020	668.0	12,1	20	12.25	14.0	2,31
2021	820.5	14,9	25	9.98	13.0	2,21
2022	955.6	17,8	29	12.25	13.2	6,23
2023	1204.5	20,0	33	8.77	12.5	8,06
2024	1457.6	24,1	38	9.8	12.0	9,97

*Determined based on expert assessment in the range from 1 to 100.

Source: Developed by the author based on data from the National Statistics Committee of the Republic of Uzbekistan and the National Agency of Perspective Projects of the Republic of Uzbekistan.

Table 5.6. Values of the regression model coefficients.

No.	Variable	Coefficient (β)	Value	Interpretation
1.	Constant (β_0)	−1.239	0.082	Not significant at 5% level
2.	Gross domestic product (*GDP*)	6.87	0.003	Valuable impact, positive
3.	Income per capita (*I*)	19.24	0.014	Significant influence
4.	Insurance culture and financial literacy (*FLI*)	42.11	0.001	High significance, strong effect
5.	Inflation (*If*)	−58.73	0.021	Negative influence
6.	Interest rate (*IR*)	36.50	0.045	Moderately positive impact

Source: Developed by the author based on data from the National Statistics Committee of the Republic of Uzbekistan and the National Agency of Perspective Projects of the Republic of Uzbekistan.

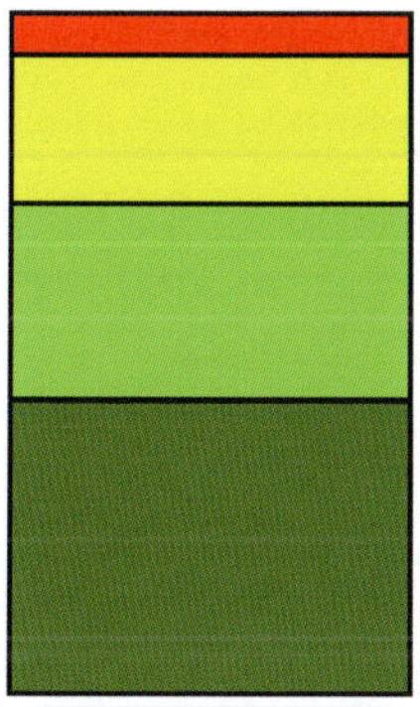

Fig. 5.10. Digitalization level of the main types of insurance activities in Uzbekistan.

The primary factors preventing the sustainable development of the insurance market in the Republic of Uzbekistan are the following barriers that hinder the active development of the industry and its integration into the country's economic system:

- insufficient level of insurance culture and awareness of insurance products among the population and business representatives;
- limited range of insurance products and lack of innovations in the development and provision of insurance services;
- low level of population coverage by insurance;
- underdeveloped compulsory insurance system;
- insufficient level of digitalization and automation processes in the insurance sector;
- shortage of qualified personnel and a lack of specialized education.

In modern conditions, the insurance culture level among representatives of the private sector, small businesses, and the general population remains at a fairly low level. Insurance culture should be understood as a conscious perception of insurance as an economically justified and necessary risk management tool. However, at the moment, most small businesses and individuals view insurance more as an additional financial burden than as a way to strengthen their own financial security. Such a perception reduces the motivation to participate in insurance programs and limits the potential of insurance as an effective tool for protection against unforeseen risks.

To overcome this barrier, a comprehensive approach to increasing the financial literacy level among the population and businesses is required. One of the key tools in this direction can be educational campaigns and programs aimed at explaining the benefits and importance of insurance. Such initiatives should be aimed at developing a conscious understanding of insurance among citizens and entrepreneurs as a mechanism that can not only reduce financial losses in case of an insurance event but also ensure the sustainability of their business or personal finances in the long term.

The limited range of insurance services offered by insurance companies in Uzbekistan is a significant obstacle to meeting both the current and future needs of various categories of clients, including legal entities and individuals. Currently, insurance companies are largely focused on basic offers, which, although providing coverage for basic risks, often do not reflect the specific needs of individual industries and socio-economic groups. Such a limitation in the range reduces the attractiveness of insurance services for potential clients and limits the ability of companies to effectively manage risks, which may vary significantly in different areas.

Insufficient diversification of insurance products is particularly notable for small- and medium-sized businesses and agricultural producers, as well as for developing environmentally sustainable and innovative sectors of the economy. For example, the small business sector requires products that take into account high liquidity risks and changes in market conditions. In agriculture, which is exposed to seasonal and climatic risks, specialized insurance products are necessary to minimize the consequences of natural disasters, crop failures, and other specific threats. In environmentally oriented and innovative sectors, such as renewable energy or green building, there is a need for products focused on insuring long-term and complex risks associated with sustainable development and the introduction of new technologies.

Expanding the range of insurance services by developing products aimed at specific needs of various sectors of the economy could significantly increase the flexibility and competitiveness of the insurance market in Uzbekistan. Diversification of offers would contribute to increased interest in insurance and attract new client groups, creating conditions for sustainable growth and improving the financial stability of both businesses and the population as a whole.

Low population coverage with insurance services is one of the key issues holding back insurance market development in Uzbekistan. This factor is confirmed by insufficient retail sales volumes of voluntary insurance types, which remain in low demand across the population. Currently, the demand for voluntary insurance products, such as life, property, health, and liability insurance, is limited largely due to a limited understanding of their value and economic feasibility. The lack of awareness among the population regarding the need for insurance as a tool for financial protection leads to many perceiving it more as an additional financial burden than as a reliable way of risk management.

One of the reasons for low demand for voluntary insurance products is again the insufficient level of public awareness of the benefits and functions of insurance. In conditions where insurance services are not widely known, consumers remain ignorant of the opportunities provided by insurance to protect their assets and financial stability. Thus, the promotion of voluntary insurance requires a comprehensive approach, including both active dissemination of information and increasing the financial literacy of the population.

To increase population coverage by voluntary insurance services, it is also necessary to simplify access to them. This can be achieved through the introduction of convenient digital platforms for the issuance and management of insurance policies and payment of insurance premiums, which will make the insurance process more accessible and less burdensome for potential clients. Simplification of procedures and development of online services can stimulate interest from the population, providing wider access to various insurance products regardless of income level or geographic location.

Insufficient development of the compulsory insurance system in Uzbekistan is a significant barrier to the formation of an effective financial protection structure in the country. Currently, there is no comprehensive compulsory insurance system, which prevents the development of such important areas as liability insurance, labor risk insurance, and property insurance against natural disasters and climate risks. The limited distribution of compulsory insurance products leads to a decrease in the level of financial protection for citizens and limits the potential of the insurance market to perform risk management functions on a national economic scale.

In conditions of insufficient coverage by compulsory insurance, especially in such key areas as insurance of labor risk and environmental liability, vulnerable population groups and priority sectors of the economy are left without reliable financial protection, which in the long term weakens social stability and security.

The development of a compulsory insurance system could help strengthen the social protection system and increase the sustainability of the insurance sector, ensuring stable income and reducing its dependence on fluctuations in voluntary insurance demand. Launching compulsory insurance types in strategically important sectors such as construction, transport, healthcare, and agriculture would help reduce economic risks and increase the responsibility of entrepreneurs toward society.

Insufficient levels of digitalization and automation of processes in the insurance sector is a significant limitation for further insurance market development in Uzbekistan. Modern global trends demonstrate the high importance of transitioning to digital solutions that can simplify the issuance of insurance policies, increase the speed and accuracy of data processing, and make client interaction more convenient and personalized. Innovations such as remote issuance and renewal of policies, real-time insurance risk management, and automated systems for insurance claims settlement are becoming an integral part of a competitive and sustainable insurance sector. However, the digitalization level in the insurance industry of Uzbekistan remains underdeveloped, creating significant barriers to the efficiency and availability of insurance services.

The lack of a full-fledged digital infrastructure and automated systems means a significant portion of the interaction between insurance companies and clients is carried out in traditional formats, requiring more time and resource costs. This factor limits the possibilities for fast and convenient customer service, which is especially important for the younger generation of users focused on digital channels. Moreover, the lack of automation leads to low data processing speed, complicates the analysis of client data, and limits the possibilities for prompt decision-making. As a result, insurance companies cannot fully adapt their offers to the individual needs of clients and respond to market changes.

Low digitalization levels also hinder the development of remote insurance, which is particularly in demand in the context of global trends toward remote work and provision of services. The ability to receive insurance services remotely would allow coverage of a wider population segment, including those in regions with limited access to insurance companies. This would also provide insurance companies with the opportunity to expand their range of services and reduce the costs related to providing services to clients through traditional channels.

Limited access to qualified personnel and a lack of specialized education in the insurance sector have a significant negative impact on the insurance market development in Uzbekistan. The personnel issue remains one of the most critical for the industry since the shortage of professionals with deep knowledge and skills in the field of insurance, risk management, and development of innovative products reduces the overall efficiency of insurance companies and customer satisfaction.

The shortage of qualified personnel leads to a decrease in the quality of customer service, which, in turn, weakens the trust of the population and businesses in insurance services. The presence of competent specialists with up-to-date knowledge of modern approaches to insurance, including issues of data analysis, actuarial calculation, and loss settlement, is a key condition for the successful functioning of an insurance company and the formation of long-term client relationships. The lack of such specialists makes it difficult not only to perform standard insurance functions but also to develop new, competitive insurance products, which is especially important in the context of growing demand for personalized and specialized services.

Shortcomings in the specialized education and training system for insurance personnel also deter the implementation of modern approaches to risk management, which reduces the adaptability and resilience of the insurance sector in the face of economic challenges. In most cases, training programs for insurance industry specialists are either absent or do not meet modern market requirements, limiting opportunities for continuous improvement of employees' qualifications. This, in turn, complicates the introduction of digital solutions and innovations necessary for successful industry development and the formation of a personnel reserve necessary for the sustainable growth of the insurance sector.

To solve this issue, a comprehensive approach is needed, including the development of specialized education and the professional training of personnel, as well as the stimulation of cooperation between insurance companies and educational institutions. The introduction of training programs aimed at training highly qualified specialists in the insurance field will allow the formation of a personnel base capable of not only satisfying current market needs but also stimulating its further development. An example is the cooperation of Uzbekinvest JSC with the National University named after M. Ulugbek and the Tashkent State Economic University.

In the context of the insurance market, the application of environmental, social, and governance (ESG) standards is becoming increasingly important due to growing demands for corporate responsibility and business sustainability in the context of global changes. For a comprehensive analysis of the ESG impact on the insurance industry, it is important to consider key aspects such as environmental sustainability, compliance with social standards, and effective governance. Table 5.7 compares these principles and their application in the insurance industry.

One of the key areas of the insurance sector development in Uzbekistan in recent years has been the introduction of the principles of environmental, social, and governance responsibility, known as ESG. In terms of the global sustainable agenda, ESG standards are strategically important, as they allow insurance companies to adapt to the growing demand for transparency, responsibility, and consideration of adverse environmental and social factors. Despite the limited practice of implementing ESG initiatives in the country, this process is becoming increasingly relevant due not only to the need to comply with international requirements but also to the need to minimize risks related to sustainability and climate change and to support socially responsible and long-term management approaches.

In Uzbekistan, the implementation of ESG standards in the insurance market involves the use of a number of strategies, including the development of environmentally oriented insurance products, the integration of sustainability criteria in risk and investment assessments, and the expansion of corporate social responsibility. For example, some insurance companies have begun to offer products focused on insuring environmental risks, which can contribute to both increasing the level of environmental protection and improving the image of companies. At the same time, insurers are developing social programs and

Table 5.7. Application of ESG standards in the insurance industry.

Criteria	General Principles	Application of ESG Standards in the Insurance Market	Examples of International and Regional Standards	Peculiarities of Application in the Insurance Industry
Environmental aspect (E)	Environmental protection, carbon footprint minimization, resilience to climate change.	Assessment and management of environmental risks and integration of sustainable principles into insurance companies' policies.	• TCFD (Task Force on Climate-related Financial Disclosures) recommendations; EU Sustainable Finance Disclosure Regulation (SFDR); UN Principles for Responsible Investment (PRI).	Insurers are required to consider environmental risks related to climate change, develop green products, and consider the impact of their investment activities on environmental sustainability.
Social aspect (S)	Human rights protection, improvement of working conditions and well-being, ethical standards observance.	Implementation of social responsibility principles through the development of insurance products oriented toward the needs of various social groups, as well as active participation in social life.	Socially responsible investments principles (SRI); ISO 26000 Social Standards	Applying social responsibility in product development, supporting inclusivity, and providing ethical conditions for employees and customers.
Governance aspect (G)	Transparency, efficiency of corporate governance, compliance with legislation and ethical standards.	Establishing strict standards of internal control, transparency in operational activities, and reporting on compliance with ESG principles.	OECD Principles of Corporate Governance; ISO 37001 standards (anti-bribery)	Insurance companies must ensure high levels of transparency, effective risk management, and corporate compliance, which helps build customer and investor confidence.
ESG integration into business models	Introduction of ESG principles at all levels of organization, including strategic planning and decision-making.	ESG factors integration into business processes, development of products that comply with ESG standards.	UN Global Compact; ISO 14001 (environmental management), ISO 45001 (occupational health and safety management)	Incorporating ESG factors into strategic planning, risk management, and insurance products development that meet sustainable practices and market requirements.
Risk assessment	Taking ESG factors into account when assessing and managing risks, especially in conditions of climate change and social responsibility.	Incorporating ESG risks into risk assessment when developing insurance products and setting rates.	• TCFD guidelines for climate risks • PRI principles for assessing social risks	Insurers should integrate ESG risk data into their risk assessment practices to help minimize potential losses and manage threats from environmental and social changes.
Transparency and reporting	Mandatory and transparent reporting on ESG principles compliance.	Developing reports that reflect the impact of insurance activities on ESG processes.	• Global Reporting Initiative GRI • CDP Carbon Footprint Standards	Insurers must publish reports that demonstrate their contribution to sustainable development and ESG commitments, which helps build confidence among investors and customers.

initiatives aimed at supporting local communities and improving the working conditions of employees, which has a positive effect on the perception of a company by society.

However, there are certain obstacles to the large-scale implementation of ESG standards in Uzbekistan. The primary challenges include the lack of qualified personnel and specialized knowledge in the field of sustainable development, the need to adapt international ESG standards to national specifics, and the lack of clear regulatory requirements governing their use in the insurance sector. Nevertheless, the prospects for the integration of ESG standards remain positive, as regulators and insurance companies increasingly recognize the importance of sustainable development as a factor contributing to long-term stability and attractiveness of the market.

The insurance market of Uzbekistan is going through a stage of active growth and transformation aimed at adapting to international standards of sustainable development. Further implementation of ESG principles will increase the sector's resilience to external challenges, improve customer and partner confidence, and strengthen the country's position in the global insurance market.

The application of ESG standards in the insurance market is a complex process that includes not only compliance with international and national regulations but also the integration of sustainable development principles into the strategy and operational activities of insurance companies. Given the global trends toward strengthening regulation in the field of sustainable finance and the growing need for transparency, insurers should actively include ESG factors in their business models. This helps both to minimize risks related to changes in the external environment and to increase the competitiveness of companies in a market focused on sustainable development.

5.2 The Role of ESG Transformation of Insurance in Achieving National Sustainable Development Goals in Uzbekistan

In the New Uzbekistan Development Strategy for 2022–2026,[2] which has been developed taking into account the Sustainable Development Goals (SDGs), the following seven priority areas of reform have been identified, aimed at further improving people's well-being, transforming economic sectors, accelerating entrepreneurship development, ensuring human rights and interests, and forming an active civil society:

- building a humane state by raising honor and human dignity and further development of a free civil society (corresponds to SDG-1, SDG-2, SDG-3, SDG-4, SDG-5, SDG-10, and SDG-16);
- transforming the principles of justice and the rule of law into a fundamental and necessary condition for the country's development (SDG 8, SDG 10, SDG 16, and SDG 17);
- accelerated development of the national economy and ensuring high growth rates (SDG-1, SDG-2, SDG-8, SDG-9, and SDG-11);
- implementing a fair social policy and human capital development (SDG-1, SDG-2, SDG-3, SDG-4, SDG-5, SDG-8, SDG-10, SDG-13, SDG-16, and SDG-17);
- ensuring spiritual development and raising this area to a new level (SDG-1, SDG-2, SDG-3, SDG-4, SDG-5, and SDG-8);
- approaching global problems with national interests in mind (SDG-6, SDG-8, SDG-9, SDG-11, SDG-12, SDG-13, SDG-15, and SDG-17);

[2] Decree of the President of the Republic of Uzbekistan dated 28.01.2022 No. UP-60 "On New Uzbekistan Development Strategy For 2022–2026". https://lex.uz/ru/docs/5841077.

- strengthening the country's security and defense potential by pursuing an open, pragmatic, and active foreign policy (SDG 8 and SDG 17).

According to a UNDP review conducted in October 2022, based on the assessment of 22 legal documents of the Republic of Uzbekistan, the level of compliance of Uzbekistan's national SDGs with the global SDGs is 79%[3] (see Fig. 5.10).

In conditions of global changes and challenges such as climate change, economic shocks, and political instability, the global economy faces the need to adapt to new realities (Fig. 5.11). In this context, increasing attention is paid to the sustainable development concept, and its integration into the economic and social sphere requires deep changes. One of the most important elements of this process is the insurance market transformation within the framework of ESG concepts. The insurance market, as an integral part of the country's financial infrastructure, plays a key role in ensuring sustainability and adaptation to global challenges. With the growing frequency and scale of natural disasters caused by climate change, as well as increased geopolitical instability, it is important to ensure effective risk management, which is directly related to the implementation of ESG principles in the insurance sector.

According to reinsurers such as Swiss Re, natural disasters cost US$270 billion in 2021, indicating the growing economic and security impact of natural disasters. This data underlines the need to rethink risk assessment approaches, especially under conditions of

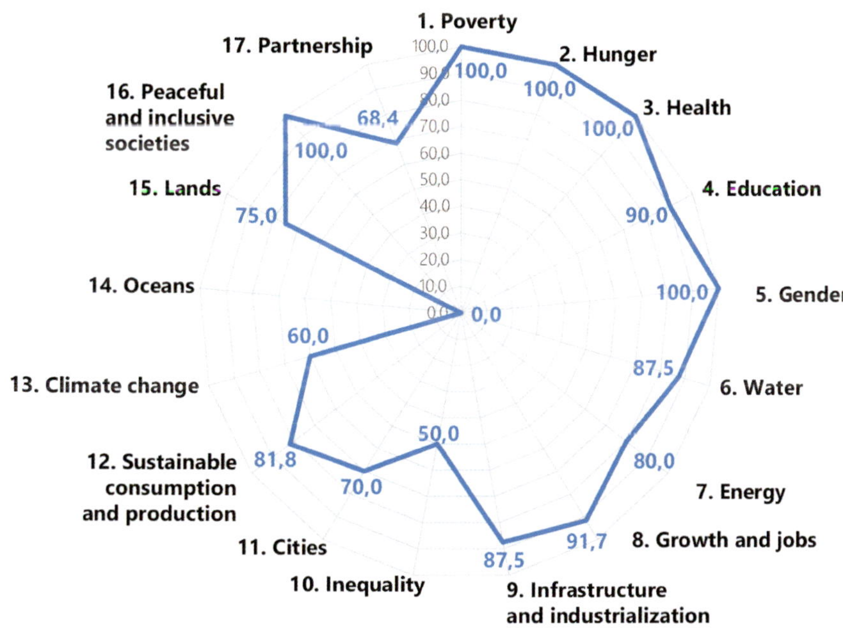

Fig. 5.11. Overall alignment of key development planning documents with global SDGs.[4]

[3]Implementing Sustainable Development Goals: Rapid Integrated Assessment of key national policy development planning documents (Uzbekistan). 19.10.2022. https://www.undp.org/uzbekistan/publications/implementing-sustainable-development-goals-rapid-integrated-assessment-key-national-policy-development-planning-documents.

[4]https://www.undp.org/uzbekistan/publications/implementing-sustainable-development-goals-rapid-integrated-assessment-key-national-policy-development-planning-documents.

climate change, and integrate sustainable practices across all levels of the insurance business.

Environmental risks related to climate change are becoming a key factor determining the insurance market's future. As part of the ESG transformation, insurers are required to take environmental factors into account in their activities, developing products and strategies that help reduce their environmental impact. This includes not only new insurance types related to protection against natural disasters but also the introduction of sustainable investment principles.

One example is the use of green bonds to finance environmentally friendly projects and initiatives. The Republic of Uzbekistan, having issued sovereign bonds in 2021 for US$235 million, used the funds to finance projects in the field of green energy and environmentally friendly transport. Insurance companies focused on ESG principles can actively participate in such projects, providing specialized insurance products and solutions for clients and investors interested in supporting sustainable development.

From a social point of view, insurers are obliged to take responsibility for human capital development and social justice. In the context of ESG, this means improving access to insurance for a wider population, supporting small- and medium-sized businesses, including women entrepreneurs, and developing products aimed at ensuring social security and well-being.

The Republic of Uzbekistan, in turn, is actively working to implement social policies aimed at improving the population's quality of life, which is reflected in various programs related to the achievement of the SDGs. Thus, within the framework of national projects, Uzbekistan allocates significant resources for the development of education, healthcare, and infrastructure, which is directly related to the social focus of insurance products.

In terms of corporate governance, insurers must apply the principles of transparency, reporting, and ethics in their activities. This is especially important in conditions of global changes and uncertainty. Insurance companies focused on sustainable development must implement mechanisms that help strengthen the trust of consumers and investors.

In the case of Uzbekistan, according to Resolution of the Cabinet of Ministers No. 83, the country has introduced additional measures to accelerate the implementation of national SDGs, which contributes to the formation of a transparent and sustainable public administration system. These measures should also be supported at the insurance sector level, which will help improve the investment climate and increase citizens' trust in financial institutions.

Integrating ESG factors into the insurance market requires attention to new risks and challenges. First of all, this concerns the development of risk assessment models that should take into account environmental and social changes occurring in the world. For example, climate change can lead to an increase in the frequency and intensity of natural disasters, which directly affects the cost of policies and payments under them. Insurance companies must develop new insurance types that will take these factors into account, as well as more actively involve the private sector in the process of implementing sustainable solutions.

At the same time, the introduction of ESG principles into the insurance market opens up new opportunities for development. For example, the development of products focused on sustainable development can attract new clients interested in environmental and social responsibility. Moreover, the use of new financial instruments, such as green and sovereign bonds, will allow attracting additional funds for the implementation of sustainable projects that will bring benefits not only to the market but also to the economy as a whole.

Thus, ESG transformation of the insurance market is a necessary step toward sustainable development in the face of global challenges. The Republic of Uzbekistan, following global trends and actively integrating sustainable development principles into its policies, is building a solid foundation for the insurance market's development, taking ESG factors into account. Insurance companies must adapt to these changes by introducing new risk assessment models and developing innovative products that contribute to the achievement of national and global SDGs.

In recent decades, sustainable development has become an important part of the global agenda. One of the key aspects of achieving sustainable development is the integration of ESG principles, known as ESG transformation, into the activities of various sectors of the economy. In a rapidly changing world and growing challenges for the environment, society, and corporate governance, the introduction of ESG principles in the insurance sector is an important step to promote national sustainable development goals.

Uzbekistan, as a country with developing economic potential, is actively integrating global sustainable development principles into its domestic policy, which opens up new opportunities for modernization and diversification of the insurance market. This part examines the role of ESG transformation of insurance in the context of achieving national sustainable development goals in Uzbekistan.

Uzbekistan, like many other countries, has signed a number of international agreements aimed at achieving the SDGs approved by the UN General Assembly in 2015. These goals cover a wide range of aspects: from fighting poverty and hunger to ensuring inclusive and sustainable economic growth, protecting the environment, and promoting social justice. Insurance, as an integral part of the financial system, plays an important role in achieving these goals.

The inclusion of ESG principles in the insurance sector is an important tool for achieving goals such as:

- **SDG 13:** Combat climate change, build resilience to natural disasters, and improve environmental safety.
- **SDG 3:** Ensure health and well-being through social and medical insurance programs.
- **SDG 16:** Promote peace and justice through improved corporate governance and the fight against corruption.

Insurance companies have significant potential to influence sustainable development. They can not only minimize financial risks but also invest in projects that promote social, environmental, and economic sustainability. With the introduction of ESG principles, insurance in Uzbekistan is becoming an important tool for ensuring protection against risks related to environmental disasters, social inequalities, and weak corporate governance.

The environmental sustainability principles in insurance imply both internal changes in companies aimed at reducing carbon footprint and improving energy efficiency and external activities aimed at reducing environmental risks for clients. In Uzbekistan, where environmental issues such as water shortages, air pollution, and land degradation are prevalent, the introduction of environmental standards in insurance can play an important role in the sustainable development of the country.

Insurance companies in Uzbekistan are beginning to actively develop green insurance, which covers risks related to environmental threats, such as:

- insurance against natural disasters (earthquakes, floods, droughts, etc.);
- environmental risk insurance for businesses operating in environmentally sensitive industries;
- financing green projects such as alternative energy, energy-efficient technologies, and environmentally friendly production processes.

In addition, increased interest in ESG investments and improved policies to reduce risks related to environmental factors contribute to building trust among clients and investors. Insurance companies can play a key role in developing financial instruments to support environmental sustainability, which in turn contributes to achieving national goals such as improving environmental quality and reducing carbon emissions.

The principles of social responsibility include improving working conditions, fighting social inequality, fostering inclusive and fair conditions for all population segments, and ensuring access to social services such as healthcare and education. In the context of insurance, this may mean developing products aimed at protecting the social and economic security of citizens, as well as integrating the principles of social justice into corporate culture.

In Uzbekistan, insurance products such as health insurance, life insurance, and social insurance are becoming increasingly popular, which helps improve social protection of the population. It is important to note that insurance companies can support the implementation of the state program on health protection and access to medical services for all segments of the population. This is especially relevant in the context of pandemic threats and changing demographics.

Other examples of social responsibility include insurance programs for low-income groups, people with disabilities, and participation in financial literacy programs. As a result of this approach, insurance becomes an important tool for social protection and helps reduce social inequality in the country.

Corporate governance in the insurance sector requires the implementation of best management practices, increased transparency, and increased trust from customers and investors. In Uzbekistan, insurance companies are gradually introducing corporate governance standards, such as:

- transparency in decision-making and reporting;
- independence and responsibility of the board of directors;
- ethical principles in business management, which include compliance with anti-corruption standards and the creation of a system for protecting the rights of clients.

The corporate governance principles in insurance contribute to improving competitiveness, increasing efficiency, and reducing risks, which is key to sustainable business development under globalization. Effective corporate governance also contributes to attracting foreign investment and improving the reputation of domestic companies in the international arena.

The introduction of ESG principles in the insurance sector of Uzbekistan is an important factor in achieving national sustainable development goals. In particular, the development of environmentally oriented insurance products and investments contributes to:

- reducing environmental risks and improving environmental quality, which is directly related to the achievement of SDG 13: Climate Action;
- ensuring social security for citizens and improving their access to social services and protection of their rights (SDG 3: Health and well-being and SDG 10: Reducing inequalities);
- strengthening corporate ethics and management transparency, which contributes to sustainable economic growth (SDG 8: Decent work and economic growth).

In addition, with the development of ESG transformation in insurance, there is an increasing interest in long-term investments aimed at sustainable development. In this context, insurance companies can become an important source of financing for green projects, social infrastructure, and innovative technologies, which will contribute to economic growth and job creation in the country.

ESG transformation of the insurance sector of Uzbekistan plays a key role in achieving national sustainable development goals. The introduction of ESG principles in the activities of insurance companies helps to solve important social and environmental problems, improve the quality of life for citizens, and increase trust in financial institutions. In the future, the continued implementation of ESG principles in insurance will allow Uzbekistan to effectively integrate into the global economy, ensuring sustainable development in the long term.

5.3 Formation of the Concept of ESG Transformation of the Domestic Insurance Business

The insurance sector, as an integral part of the country's financial system, plays a key role in economic development and the social protection of the population. In recent years, the world, particularly developing economies such as Uzbekistan, has seen a growing interest in the principles of ESG transformation. With emerging global challenges such as climate change, social inequality, and economic and financial crises, the need to implement ESG principles in the insurance sector has become especially urgent. This is due to both the desire for sustainable economic growth and the increasing need for social and environmental protection of the population and businesses.

For the domestic insurance business, an important step in response to the challenges of modern times is the development and implementation of the ESG transformation concept. Effective integration of ESG principles into the activities of insurance companies can become the basis for increasing their competitiveness, sustainability, and social responsibility. This section considers the formation of the ESG transformation concept of the domestic insurance business in the context of implementing national sustainable development goals and ensuring long-term financial stability.

ESG transformation is the process of integrating sustainability, social responsibility, and corporate governance principles into a company's strategy and operations. In the insurance business, this process includes not only improving the quality and availability of insurance products but also developing a corporate strategy focused on sustainability, risk minimization, improvement of stakeholder engagement, and support for environmental and social initiatives.

The main goals of ESG transformation in insurance are:

- minimization of environmental risks through the development of green insurance products such as natural catastrophe insurance, green investment insurance, and support for sustainable technologies;
- ensuring social responsibility through the development of medical and social insurance programs and participation in projects aimed at supporting vulnerable population groups;
- improving corporate governance through increased transparency, business ethics, and effective compliance with risk management standards, which contributes to increased confidence among customers and investors.

The implementation of ESG principles helps insurance companies strengthen their market positions; it also makes a significant contribution to achieving the SDGs, such as fighting climate change, improving the health and well-being of the population, and building effective governance institutions and business practices.

Before formulating an ESG transformation framework, it is necessary to analyze the current state of the insurance market of Uzbekistan and assess the industry's readiness to implement ESG principles.

Today, the insurance market of Uzbekistan continues to develop, and in recent years, positive dynamics in its growth have been observed. However, many insurance companies have not yet fully integrated ESG principles into their activities. This is due to the following factors:

- lack of awareness of the importance of ESG principles for business and society;
- low integration of environmental and social factors in decision-making processes, which limits the possibilities for reducing the risks related to climate change and social instability;
- lack of effective tools for the assessment and management of ESG risks, which reduces the attractiveness of insurance companies for potential investors.

Despite the above, there are a number of factors that can contribute to the successful ESG transformation of the insurance sector in Uzbekistan, including:

- legislative initiatives and reforms aimed at improving financial regulation and attracting foreign investment, which contributes to the development of more sustainable business practices;
- growing interest in sustainable investing, which provides a base for the development of green insurance products;
- reduction of environmental risks caused by natural disasters, as well as growing attention to social issues such as access to healthcare and protection from poverty.

Thus, at the current development stage of the insurance industry in Uzbekistan, there is significant potential for the implementation of ESG principles, but it requires a comprehensive strategy and adaptation of existing business models to the requirements of sustainable development.

The formation of the ESG transformation concept for the domestic insurance business should be based on a number of key areas that will allow integrating ESG responsibility into the strategy and activities of insurance companies. These areas can be divided into three main categories: environmental sustainability, social responsibility, and governance efficiency.

As part of environmental sustainability, insurance companies must develop products aimed at minimizing environmental risks and supporting sustainable development. Key areas may include the following:

- **Insurance against natural disasters:** With the increasing frequency of extreme weather phenomena (floods, earthquakes, and droughts), it is required to develop insurance against risks related to climate change.
- **Green insurance:** This includes developing products for companies, implementing sustainable technologies, and complying with environmental standards.
- **Investments in green projects:** Insurance companies can become important players in the market for environmentally friendly and sustainable projects, including financing alternative energy sources and carbon-reducing technologies.

Insurance should play an important role in the social protection of citizens, ensuring access to quality medical services and social programs. The main areas of social responsibility include the following:

- **Medical and social insurance:** Product development should aim at improving the availability of medical services, health insurance, and life insurance for citizens.
- **Programs for the vulnerable population groups:** This involves the inclusion of insurance products that promote social integration of disabled, retired, unemployed, and other vulnerable categories of citizens.
- **Support for financial literacy programs:** Educational programs aimed at raising public awareness of the possibilities of insurance and its role in social protection should be conducted.

To effectively implement ESG principles, it is necessary to introduce best corporate governance practices that will ensure transparency and responsibility of insurance companies:

- **Increasing the level of transparency and reporting:** Insurance companies must publish detailed reports on their activities, including in terms of environmental and social responsibility.
- **Implementing anti-corruption standards:** Ethics and good faith at all levels of business can reduce corruption risks.
- **Forming independent and effective governing bodies:** Formation of independent boards of directors is essential for ensuring transparency in strategic decision-making.

To successfully implement ESG transformation in the domestic insurance sector, it is necessary to go through several key stages:

1. **Assessing the current state and developing a strategy:** At this first stage, it is necessary to carry out an analysis of the current state of insurance companies, determine the degree of their readiness to implement ESG principles, and formulate an ESG transformation strategy.
2. **Development of new products and services:** Based on the strategy, new insurance products aimed at sustainable development are to be developed, such as insurance against risks related to climate change, green insurance, and medical and social programs.
3. **Integration of ESG principles into corporate governance:** This involves implementing corporate governance standards, training staff and providing guidance on ESG principles, and conducting regular impact assessments of ESG initiatives.
4. **Monitoring and reporting:** This includes continuous monitoring the implementation of ESG strategies, data collection and analysis of implementation results, and publication of reports for stakeholders.

The formation of the ESG transformation concept for domestic insurance businesses is an important step toward sustainable economic development and social protection of the population. The introduction of ESG responsibility into the strategy and activities of insurance companies in Uzbekistan will not only increase their competitiveness and resilience to external risks but also significantly improve the quality of life for citizens, contribute to solving environmental problems, and strengthen confidence in the financial sector. For a

Table 5.8. Comparison of global ESG practices in insurance.

Country/Region	Environmental Responsibility (E)	Social Responsibility (S)	Corporate Governance (G)
European Union	• Green insurance development for businesses and individuals (environmental insurance, insurance against natural disasters). • Investments in sustainable energy projects. • Inclusion of climate risks in the assessment of insurance products.	• Development of socially responsible products, including health and pension insurance. • Inclusive insurance programs for vulnerable groups (retired, disabled people, and migrants).	• Strict requirements for information disclosure on ESG factors (e.g. within the SFDR). • Application of high standards of corporate ethics and anti-corruption policies.
USA	• Insurance against environmental risks related to climate change (fires, floods, hurricanes, etc.). • Assessing the impact of environmental risks on assets and projects (through sustainable investments).	• Widening access to health and social programs. • Inclusion of the principles of inclusiveness and consumer protection.	• Mandatory ESG reports, including for institutional investors (e.g. SEC). • Increased attention to transparency and risk management issues in the company.
UK	• Development of products focused on climate risks (insurance against natural disasters). • Insurance of "green" assets and sustainable business models.	• Programs for the protection of consumer rights and the disabled. • Implementation of insurance with a social responsibility component.	• High level of corporate responsibility and transparency. • Implementation of principles of sustainable corporate governance through independent boards of directors.
Australia	• Assessment of climate risks and implementation of green insurance products for business (catastrophic risk insurance). • Support for climate change and sustainable development initiatives.	• Development and distribution of health and pension insurance programs for low-income groups.	• Developed practice of ESG information disclosure (through climate reports and standard reporting forms). • Ensuring high transparency in corporate decisions.
Japan	• Insurance against natural disasters (earthquakes, tsunamis, etc.), which is related to the risks of climate change.	• Inclusiveness in social programs: health insurance, support for vulnerable groups.	• Use of strict corporate standards to manage risks and ensure business sustainability.
China	• Increasing investments in sustainable development projects, including through environmental insurance products.	• Active development of social insurance programs, including pension and medical.	• Strict government regulation and supervision of companies' actions in the field of risk management and reporting.

Table 5.9. Comparison of the ESG principles implementation in insurance in different countries.

Parameter/Country	European Union	USA	UK	Japan
Green Insurance Products	Development of green insurance policies (e.g. climate change insurance).	Climate risk-focused products (hurricane and flood insurance) are widespread.	Natural disaster and environmental damage insurance programs.	Natural disaster insurance, especially earthquakes and tsunamis.
Social Programs	Health and social insurance programs for vulnerable groups.	Health insurance through government and private programs (e.g. Obamacare).	Pension and health programs that support inclusion.	Developing programs for the aging population and people with disabilities.
Corporate Governance	Transparency and disclosure of ESG information (e.g. through SFDR).	SEC requires ESG reporting for public companies.	Mandatory climate risk reporting for financial institutions.	Introducing standards for corporate governance through supervisory bodies.
State Initiatives	Strong sustainability regulation, support for green bonds.	Legislative initiatives on environmental disclosure and reporting (e.g. SEC).	Strict government sustainability policies.	Supporting sustainable investments, creating environmental standards for business.

detailed illustration of the ESG transformation concept of the insurance business of Uzbekistan in the context of international practice, it is possible to use comparative tables that will help in clearly demonstrating how global ESG practices are integrated into the insurance industry's development and what lessons might be useful for Uzbekistan.

A comparison of ESG principles implementation in insurance in different countries is described in Table 5.9.

An example of ESG principles implementation at the level of insurance companies is given in Table 5.10.

For a successful ESG transformation of the insurance business of Uzbekistan, several key strategies based on international experience can be identified:

1. **Development of green insurance products:** Uzbekistan can activate the development of climate-sensitive products, including insurance against natural disasters (floods, earthquakes, and droughts) and those that support sustainable development projects (e.g. green insurance for agriculture).
2. **Development of socially oriented products:** It is important to expand access to health and pension insurance for vulnerable groups such as the retired, people with disabilities, and low-income groups. Developing products that promote financial inclusion will also be an important element.
3. **Increase transparency and reporting:** Introduction of mandatory ESG reporting standards and publication of data on companies' impact on social and environmental factors will help to build a sustainable system of trust among consumers and investors. This should include both environmental reporting and information on social responsibility and ethics in governance.
4. **Integration of ESG into corporate culture:** It is important to develop internal management practices that will take into account not only financial performance but also sustainability factors, including climate risk management, anti-corruption standards, and ethical business practices.

Table 5.10. Example of the ESG principles implementation at the level of insurance companies.

Company	Environmental Responsibility (E)	Social Responsibility (S)	Corporate Governance (G)
Allianz (Germany)	• Providing green insurance for sustainable construction and energy. • Investments in renewable energy sources.	• Programs to extend the availability of health insurance for low-income people.	• Active work to ensure transparency of reporting on ESG factors. • Ethical principles in management.
AXA (France)	• Insurance of risks related to climate change and natural disasters. • Development of "green" investment products.	• Health programs for vulnerable groups. • Support for women's rights and inclusion.	• Implementation of strict standards for ESG reporting and transparency.
Prudential (UK)	• Investments in environmentally friendly projects. • Programs for insurance against natural risks.	• Programs for the elderly and people with disabilities.	• Management through independent boards of directors, strict risk assessment and control procedures.
Tokyo Marine (Japan)	• Insurance against natural disasters, including earthquakes and tsunamis.	• Health and pension insurance programs for the aging population.	• Transparency of reporting and use of corporate standards for risk management.

The introduction of ESG principles in the insurance business of Uzbekistan is an important step toward sustainable development and increasing the competitiveness of the industry. Studying global practices and successful examples, such as the use of green insurance products in Europe and the United States, allows us to formulate a number of strategic directions that will contribute not only to the economic sustainability of insurance companies but also to social and environmental responsibility. Uzbekistan has every opportunity to develop an insurance market based on these recommendations, which will contribute to the achievement of national sustainable development goals.

5.4 Conclusions

1. The insurance market of Uzbekistan demonstrates stable growth but retains features of institutional immaturity: low indicators of insurance density and coverage imply a fragmented structure. Digitalization is developing but is limited by regulatory and infrastructural barriers; the implementation of ESG practices has begun but is hampered by a shortage of qualified personnel, a methodological base, and information resources.

   Long-term sustainability of the sector requires systematic changes: expansion of compulsory insurance in key industries, active digital transformation, institutionalization of ESG standards, and development of educational partnerships. Without regulation, modernization, and full integration of sustainable development principles, further growth will remain fragmented and insufficiently aligned with the global sustainable finance agenda.
2. ESG transformation of the insurance sector of Uzbekistan is an integral element of systematic adaptation to global challenges and a factor in sustainable socio-economic development. Integrating ESG principles into insurance activities enhances the insurance potential as a tool for risk management, sustainable investment mobilization, and social protection of the population. In the context of the implementation of the National Development Strategy and with a high degree of consistency with the global SDGs, the insurance market is becoming an important instrument for supporting economic sustainability, social inclusiveness, and environmental safety. Thus, ESG approaches in insurance act not only as corporate ethics but also as a strategic basis for the modernization of the financial infrastructure of Uzbekistan in the context of sustainable development.
3. The formation of the ESG transformation concept in Uzbek insurance businesses is a strategically significant vector for the modernization of the republic's financial system, focused on sustainable development. The integration of ESG principles into the activities of insurance companies is motivated by both global challenges and internal needs to improve social protection, reduce climate risks, and strengthen institutional sustainability. Despite the current institutional and methodological limitations, the insurance sector of the republic has the necessary potential to adapt to the ESG paradigm. Systematic implementation of ESG principles will not only strengthen the competitiveness of the insurance market but also increase its contribution to the achievement of national and international sustainable development goals.

Conclusion

This study on environmental, social, and governance (ESG) transformation in insurance, with a special focus on countries with transition economies, particularly the Republic of Uzbekistan, aims to identify key factors that influence the implementation of sustainable development principles in this important economic sector. Given the growing attention of the global community to sustainable development issues, the implementation of ESG in insurance is becoming not only relevant but also a necessary step to ensure long-term financial sustainability, increase corporate responsibility, and enhance resilience to external risks. The study examined international practices and also conducted a detailed analysis of the current state of the insurance sector in Uzbekistan and its potential for integrating ESG principles.

Global practices of implementing sustainable development principles in insurance show that ESG components are becoming important indicators influencing the ability of insurance companies to attract investment, reduce operational risks, and enhance their competitiveness. In countries with developed economies, the use of ESG approaches in insurance is not only aimed at complying with legislation and market requirements but also serves as an additional factor in enhancing the reputation of companies. The use of ESG standards in the insurance business includes both internal processes – corporate governance, ethical practices, and respect for human rights – and external impact related to environmental sustainability and social responsibility.

International examples, such as the introduction of "green" insurance products in the European Union and the active participation of leading global insurance companies in the initiative to finance environmentally friendly projects, serve as vivid illustrations of successful ESG practices. At the same time, in countries with transition economies, such as Uzbekistan, the experience of implementing ESG is limited due to differences in legislative and economic conditions, as well as insufficient awareness and readiness of local market participants for such changes.

In Uzbekistan, the insurance sector, although demonstrating stable growth, has not yet been covered by large-scale reforms aimed at the implementation of ESG principles. Key problems preventing the implementation of these initiatives are: insufficient regulatory framework development, the lack of information on the principles of sustainable development among market participants, and the lack of appropriate tools for integrating ESG into the insurance process.

However, there is a steady trend in the country toward modernization of the financial sector and improvement of its interaction with international partners. This fact creates potential for the ESG introduction in insurance. The strategic role of the state, actively supporting digitalization and sustainable development, as well as the participation of large financial and insurance companies in international initiatives, can become a powerful incentive for the formation of a favorable regulatory framework and the stimulation of sustainable practices at the corporate governance level.

One of the key benefits of implementing ESG in insurance is the opportunity to increase transparency and trust from clients and investors. The use of ESG standards contributes to the formation of more sustainable and less risky business models. In conditions of growing climate risks, social changes, and the need for responsible investments, insurance companies focused on ESG principles will be able not only to minimize risks but also to access new sources of capital, including through green and social bonds.

In addition, the development of sustainable business models will contribute to improving the social climate since many ESG initiatives include support for social projects and respect for human rights. This will help strengthen the image of Uzbekistan as a responsible member of the global community, opening up new opportunities for foreign investors.

Despite the opportunities, the implementation of sustainable development principles in insurance in Uzbekistan faces several significant obstacles. First, there is currently a shortage of legislative and regulatory acts governing ESG use in the insurance industry. The lack of clear standards for assessing ESG risks and the underdeveloped reporting system limit opportunities for effective implementation of these principles.

Secondly, in practice, there are significant difficulties in adapting insurance products and services to ESG requirements. Companies face a shortage of specialists capable of developing and implementing ESG strategies, as well as difficulties in finding and implementing innovative solutions in the field of sustainable insurance. The market is also limited in terms of available financial instruments focused on sustainable development.

For the successful introduction of ESG into the insurance sector of Uzbekistan, it is necessary to focus on several key areas:

- Development of the legislative and regulatory framework: Development and introduction of standards for ESG reporting and risk assessment in insurance will help ensure transparency and uniformity of practices among all market participants. It will also provide impetus for the wider adoption of ESG strategies in the industry.
- Raising awareness and professional training: It is important to organize educational programs and trainings for employees of insurance companies and investors aimed at developing competencies in the field of sustainable development and ESG practices.
- Creating incentives for the application of ESG products: Insurance companies can develop products aimed at maintaining the sustainability of ecosystems, such as climate change risk insurance or insurance for social initiatives. This will require not only innovative approaches but also support from the state, including subsidies or tax incentives.

Key Research Conclusions

1. **The necessity to implement ESG in the insurance sector Uzbekistan:** In recent decades, there has been a growing interest in the principles of sustainable development at the global level. Countries with developing economies, including Uzbekistan, face challenges related to the need to integrate ESG principles into their business practices. This is due to both changes in international regulatory policies and growing demands from investors and clients focused on social responsibility and long-term sustainability. The ESG introduction in insurance, as in other areas of the economy, is becoming an important step toward increasing corporate responsibility, improving reputation, and ensuring transparency of business processes.

In particular, the transition to sustainable insurance helps reduce risks related to climate and social change, which in turn helps to strengthen trust both on the part of clients and on the part of international partners and investors. For insurers, the implementation of ESG principles provides an opportunity to expand access to international financial markets, attracting investments focused on environmentally and socially responsible projects. In addition, companies that actively apply ESG standards have new prospects for developing products and services that meet sustainable development requirements, which strengthens their competitiveness in the market.

2. **Opportunities for ESG implementation in the insurance sector of Uzbekistan:** The Republic of Uzbekistan has a number of factors that can become the basis for the successful integration of ESG principles into the insurance sector. Among the most significant opportunities are the following:
   - Increasing government regulation in the area of sustainable development: In recent years, the government of Uzbekistan has been actively focusing efforts on modernizing its economy and improving the investment climate. The development and implementation of an effective regulatory framework in the field of sustainable development will be an important step in supporting ESG implementation in insurance. Legislative regulation will facilitate the development of transparent and understandable standards, allowing insurers to adapt their practices to ESG requirements.
   - Increasing the financial literacy level of the population and awareness of the importance of eco-social factors: Effective implementation of ESG in insurance is impossible without raising awareness among the population regarding the importance of environmental and social aspects in making financial decisions. Educational programs aimed at improving financial literacy, as well as familiarization with the principles of sustainable development, will help to raise awareness among both potential clients and insurance market participants.
   - The strategic role of international financial institutions: Uzbekistan actively cooperates with international financial organizations such as the World Bank and the Asian Development Bank. These organizations provide both technical and financial assistance in implementing projects aimed at sustainable development. The introduction of ESG principles in insurance can become part of broader initiatives to modernize and transform the country's economy, supported by international financial institutions.
   - Active participation of insurance companies: Important players in the insurance market are the insurance companies that can become catalysts for ESG implementation in this sector. The participation of such organizations in initiatives aimed at sustainable development will contribute to the formation of positive experiences and the demonstration of successful practices based on the example of market leaders. Strategies aimed at integrating ESG can be further strengthened through public–private partnerships, which will ensure stability and effective interaction of all participants in the process.
3. **Obstacles and challenges to the ESG implementation in Uzbekistan:** Despite the existence of significant opportunities for ESG implementation in the insurance sector of Uzbekistan, the transformation process faces a number of obstacles that need to be overcome. The main challenges include the following:
   - Insufficient development of the legislative and regulatory framework: Currently, Uzbekistan lacks a clearly defined legislative framework governing the sustainable development principles in the insurance sector. This complicates the implementation of ESG standards at the level of insurance companies since the lack of

regulation leads to uncertainty in matters of compliance of corporate practices with international standards of sustainable development. The development and implementation of regulations governing ESG implementation in insurance is an important step in forming a reliable legal framework

- Lack of clear standards and indicators for assessment of ESG risks and opportunities: In Uzbekistan, standard methods for assessing ESG risks and indicators have not yet been developed, which complicates their application in practice. This prevents the development of new insurance products based on sustainable and environmentally friendly initiatives and also reduces interest from investors who are unable to objectively assess ESG risks and their impact on a company's financial results.
- Insufficient level of trust from the insureds: In the initial stage of implementing ESG principles, there is a problem with trust from end users – insureds. Successful ESG implementation in insurance requires developing an understanding among clients about the benefits and importance of sustainable insurance, as well as providing transparent information on how these principles can affect risk reduction and increase the value of services.
- Limited possibilities for adapting existing business models and practices: Insurance companies in Uzbekistan, as in other countries with transition economies, face limitations in adapting their business models to new requirements. Existing structures and practices focused on traditional approaches to risk management require significant changes to be compatible with ESG approaches. This includes changes not only at the level of operational processes but also at the level of corporate culture and approaches to interaction with clients.

The introduction of ESG principles in the insurance sector of Uzbekistan is a promising but complex process requiring a comprehensive approach and coordination of efforts by government agencies, financial institutions, the business community, and the public. At the same time, proper regulation, development of educational programs, support for international initiatives, and active participation of key players in the economy can create opportunities for the successful implementation of ESG principles in the country. Solving the above challenges will open new horizons for insurance sector development, improve its resilience to external risks, and contribute to the formation of more responsible and sustainable businesses in the long term.

Proposals for Further Research and Practical Application

1. **Development of the regulatory framework and ESG standards:** One of the primary tasks for the successful integration of sustainable development principles into the insurance sector of Uzbekistan is the development of a clear regulatory framework governing ESG practices in this industry. The need to develop such standards is due to the current lack of a unified system for assessing ESG risks and opportunities, which hinders the creation of transparent reporting and effective control over their implementation. In this context, it is important not only to develop national standards for insurance companies but also to adapt international experience and best practices, which will ensure compatibility with global requirements and expand opportunities for attracting international investment.

   The development of such standards should include criteria for assessing and monitoring ESG risks that would take into account all ESG factors affecting the sustainability of the insurance business. It is important to provide a mechanism for their mandatory application and regular reporting in order to guarantee a high degree of transparency and responsibility from the insurance market participants. In this regard, it also seems relevant to introduce a certification system that would assess the compliance level of companies with the adopted ESG standards.

2. **Training and raising awareness:** One of the key success factors in the process of implementing ESG in the insurance sector is raising awareness and training personnel. To do this, it is necessary to develop educational programs aimed at training specialists both in the field of insurance and in the field of sustainable development. It is important to develop courses and training for employees of insurance companies, which will study sustainable development principles, methods for assessing ESG risks, and practical tools for implementing ESG in corporate management and operational processes.

   Additionally, information campaigns should be conducted to raise awareness among clients and the general public about the importance of applying ESG principles in insurance. This will not only improve understanding of the benefits of sustainable development for business but also contribute to demand growth for environmentally and socially oriented insurance products. Clients' awareness of the impact of their choices on the insurance companies' sustainability will play an important role in accelerating the adoption of ESG approaches.
3. **Client initiatives and innovations in insurance:** The introduction of ESG principles into insurance opens up opportunities for the development of new products and services focused on sustainable development. Insurance companies can offer customers innovative products that meet the needs of protecting ecosystems, improving social welfare, or ensuring workers' rights. For example, the development of environmental insurance that covers risks related to climate change or products aimed at supporting social projects and ensuring social responsibility will be an important step in the market transformation.

   The inclusion of innovative insurance types in the product line, such as insurance against environmental risks, compensation for damage from natural disasters, or the development of insurance programs to support corporate social responsibility, will help attract a new client base interested in supporting sustainable initiatives. Such products can be supported by government initiatives or subsidies, which will increase their availability and attractiveness to a wide range of clients.
4. **Investing in sustainable infrastructure:** The implementation of ESG principles in the insurance sector of Uzbekistan is not limited to changes in insurance products; it also requires a review of investment strategies of companies. Insurance companies should actively develop and implement strategies for investing in sustainable projects, including environmentally friendly and socially responsible initiatives. In particular, this may apply to the financing of green bonds, carbon emission reduction projects, and social infrastructure, as well as projects in the field of renewable energy and ecotourism.

   Developing specialized investment portfolios focused on projects with high ESG ratings will be an important step in integrating sustainable principles into financial activities. Such an approach will not only support the transition to sustainable development but will also help reduce investment risks related to environmental and social changes. It is also important to develop cooperation with international financial institutions, such as the World Bank, which can provide the necessary financial and technical support for the implementation of these strategies.
5. **Monitoring and evaluation of ESG implementation:** To ensure effective and consistent implementation of ESG principles in the insurance sector, it is necessary to develop a system for monitoring and assessing the impact of these changes on the

economy and society. Regular monitoring will help identify the most successful practices and approaches that can be extended to other companies and market segments, as well as promptly identify issues and obstacles in the transformation process. This will also help track the impact of ESG initiatives on companies' financial results, their reputation, and their attractiveness in international markets.

It is important to implement a system for the independent assessment of the effectiveness of ESG practices in insurance companies, which will ensure a higher degree of trust from investors and clients. Such monitoring may include regular audits and independent checks that will ensure compliance with established standards and regulations. Publication of monitoring results in the form of reports will help increase the level of transparency and responsibility of insurance market participants.

Effective implementation of sustainable development principles in the insurance sector of Uzbekistan requires a comprehensive approach, including legislative initiatives, educational programs, the development of new products, and investment strategies. It is important that all stakeholders actively interact in this process: government agencies, financial institutions, insurance companies, and civil society. Development of infrastructure for ESG implementation, creation of control mechanisms, and support from international organizations will ensure the successful integration of sustainable practices into insurance, which will contribute to the long-term development of both the sector itself and the economy as a whole.

Further Reading

Alesina, A. and Spolaore, E. (2003). The size of nations.
Aslund, A. (2007). How Russia became a market economy.
Baek, P. (2001). Economic reforms and financial stability in Central Asia: A comparative analysis.
Cummings, S. N. and Lewis, A. (2003). Post-Soviet economic reforms in Central Asia: A case study approach.
Davies, P. and Ginsburg, N. (2000). Financial sector reform in Central Asia.
Grigoriev, G. (1999). Economic reforms in the CIS countries: The challenges of transition.
Kasyimov, A. (2003). Economic growth and structural transformation in Central Asia.
Kaufmann, D., Kraay, A. and Mastruzzi, M. (2009). Governance matters VII.
Lahti, M. L. (2002). Transition and institutional change in Central Asia.
Pomfret, R. (2006). The economics of Central Asia.
Rajan, R. G. and Zingales, L. (2003). The capitalistic spirit.
Rakhimov, S. (2004). Economic reform and the role of government in Central Asia.
Rashid, A. (2002). The resurgence of Central Asia: Islam, nationalism, and politics.
Shymberdiyev, K. (2006). The economic transition of Kazakhstan: Challenges and opportunities.
Stiglitz, J. E. (2002). Globalization and its discontents.
Ekonomika Tsentral'noy Azii: novyy vzglyad [Economy of Central Asia: A New Look.] https://eabr.org/upload/iblock/d0b/EDB_2022_Report-3_The-Economy-of-CA_rus.pdf.
Disaster Property Insurance in Uzbekistan: Overview and Recommendations https://documents1.worldbank.org/curated/en/617231591599422910/pdf/Disaster-Property-Insurance-in-Uzbekistan-Overview-and-Recommendations.pdf.
European Insurance and Occupational Pensions Authority (EIOPA) https://european-union.europa.eu/institutions-law-budget/institutions-and-bodies/search-all-eu-institutions-and-bodies/european-insurance-and-occupational-pensions-authority-eiopa_en.
https://www.allstate.com/.
https://www.statefarm.com/.
https://www.lemonade.com/.
https://www.docusign.com/.
https://www.adobe.com/sign.html.
Allianz Builds a Future-Ready Business with Intelligent Automation. https://www.blueprism.com/resources/case-studies/allianz-builds-a-future-ready-business-with-intelligent-automation/.
https://careers.axa.com/global/en/job/AXGRGLOBAL180006XDYESTALEOENEXTERNALENGLOBAL/Robotics-Process-Automation-Assistant-Manager.
https://aigautomation.co.uk/.
Decree of the President of the Republic of Uzbekistan dated January 28, 2022 N UP-60. "On the New Uzbekistan Development Strategy for 2022–2026". https://lex.uz/ru/docs/5841077.
Implementing Sustainable Development Goals: Rapid Integrated Assessment of key national policy development planning documents (Uzbekistan) October 19, 2022. https://www.undp.org/uzbekistan/publications/implementing-sustainable-development-goals-rapid-integrated-assessment-key-national-policy-development-planning-documents.

Index